GENERATION Y

and the

NEW

RULES *of* MANAGEMENT

MARK MURPHY

with ANDREA BURGIO-MURPHY

Founders of Leadership IQ

ISBN   978-1-60013-283-4

Publishing by
INSIGHT PUBLISHING
647 Wall Street • Sevierville, Tennessee • 37862

10 9 8 7 6 5 4 3 2 1

in dedication…

For Isabella and Andrew

Table of Contents

Introduction

CRU >< by yung wrkrz hu feel ntitld 2 6S, nd constant kudos, wnt evryting 2B "their wA" n may evn dr$ lk vagabonds? RU strugglin 2 attract n retain a gNR8N of wrkrz hus commitment sEmz mor temp thN perm? dis S gNR8N Y, a wrk4S of as mnE as 70 million, n d 1st ~~~ S jst nyt takN their plce n an incrsngly mulTgNR8NL wrkplce.

*Y*ou're looking at text talk; the language of Generation Y, and if you have no idea what it says, you're not alone. These former Babies-on-Board are growing up and going to work. And their personal shorthand isn't the only generational clash to hit the workplace. Gen Y has vastly different demands, expectations and motivators than the generations that came before them. The old rules of management are no longer effective, and the best leaders are embracing the change. They're focused on finding out what makes Gen Y tick and creating a new set of rules to attract, retain, manage and motivate this new generation of talent.

The situation isn't entirely unique. Every new generation has entered the job market with ideas and beliefs that challenge, and often change, how leaders manage their workforce. But Gen Y is pushing the envelope harder and faster than ever. They may be young, but they're also self-assured and bold, and their comfort with technology gives them a definite edge. They're not bashful when it comes to asking for what they want. And if you tell them no, they want to know why not. Unlike past generations, Gen Y has options, and they're not afraid to hold out—or bail out—for an employer of choice.

Regardless of whether you think Gen Y is changing the rules or breaking them, there's no turning back. Gen Y isn't just a passing fad or a challenge to be tackled and forgotten. In fact, they're a sign of things to come. The boundaries that define a generation are getting narrower as the speed of the world increases. It used be 30 years before a new generation jumped on to the work scene and shook up the status quo. These days it's more like ten, and soon it will be five or less. And leaders who cling to the old rules and refuse to adapt to the inevitable are going to find themselves out of the game.

The good news is that you don't have to learn a whole new language to manage Gen Y. You just need to change a few rules and create a balance between what the younger generation wants and what your organization is willing and able to give. The new rules aren't about coddling Gen Y or giving them something for nothing. Quite the opposite, it's leaders who stand to gain the most from the new rules. These teaching tools are built around the attributes, values and experiences that shaped this young generation. And when you learn to use the words and actions that resonate and inspire Gen Y to be the best they can be, the benefit will be all yours.

Gen Y may not operate in the work environment the same way as preceding generations, but that doesn't mean they don't want to work. They just want to work differently. The best of the bunch has what it takes to lead the way into the future. And the future of your organization depends on them. They deserve the opportunity to prove what they can do, but they need strong leadership to get there. And the key to harnessing the talent of these twenty-somethings lies in understanding and addressing the differences.

Companies like Nike, Google and Apple have already made the leap. They figured out how to reach the younger generation with a leadership style that communicates the choices and opportunities Gen Y seeks. Not only have these organizations successfully leveraged their younger employee's high performer potential, they've also gained a name in the Gen Y culture as being a great place to work. And in an era of increasing transparency and viral networking, that's a reputation that's worth its weight in gold.

Don't make the mistake of thinking your organization needs to be a household name with money to burn in order to give Gen Y what they want. They're not looking for a million bucks or a corner office. And despite their reputation for wanting to get ahead in a hurry, once you explain to them what being the boss actually entails, they probably won't want your job either; at least not today. The things they do want are fairly easy to produce and deliver, if you're willing to make some changes.

Leadership IQ has taught the techniques behind the Generation Y and the New Rules of Management to thousands of companies around the world through our seminars and Webinars. We've seen individual leaders and entire organizations transform the approach they take with their Gen Y employees to achieve remarkable results in very little time. And now, you can too. All it takes is an open mind and a willingness to make it happen.

Oh, and if you're still wondering about that gibberish up above, here's the translation:

> *Are you frustrated by young workers who feel entitled to success, need constant praise, want everything to be "their way" and may even dress like vagabonds? Are you struggling to attract and retain a generation of workers whose commitment seems more temporary than permanent? This is Generation Y, a workforce of as many as 70 million, and the first wave is just now taking their place in an increasingly multigenerational workplace.*

Download free tools for managing Generation Y at:
www.generationy.net

Learn about Leadership IQ's training programs at:
www.leadershipiq.com

Gen Y High Performer or High Maintenance?

efore we get started with the new rules, we first need to address what has become a widespread debate: are Gen Yers the next breed of high performer or are they just high maintenance? On the one side are the folks, like us, who say if you meet the younger generation halfway, you can lead them to greatness. The other side begs to differ. They're angry, and the mere mention of Gen Y typically inspires a verbal out lash that includes some pretty unflattering generalizations. You've probably heard something along the lines of: Gen Yers are mollycoddled over privileged super indulged brats who are lazy, insolent, arrogant, and disloyal. And God help you if you don't praise them just for showing up to work.

Feeling anger towards Gen Y is an honest emotion. So if you find yourself letting off a little steam, you're in good company. Most of us have a natural inclination to fight change, especially when it's not our idea and it challenges our core values and beliefs. Throw in personal inconvenience and you'll likely be the odd man out if you don't get at least a little rattled. And we're the first to admit that Gen Y fits the bill on all counts. After all, who are these kids marching into our workplaces and telling us we need to change the way we do things?

But getting angry at Gen Y won't alter reality or make them magically transform into something they're not. And defining a generation of 70 million plus with a sweeping generalization is simply unrealistic. Because let's face it, every generation has had its share of slackers, but they've also produced a lot of valuable high performers. And Gen Y is no different. The rules may have changed, but the job hasn't. Great leadership still means gaining the trust and loyalty of your people so they do what you want. And common sense dictates that anger isn't going to help achieve that goal.

Tension between the generations typically stems from perception. For older generation leaders it usually boils down to work ethic and respect: two factors in which some managers deem Gen Y to be seriously lacking. Take David, for example, a 50 year-old senior level executive in charge of marketing for a national food distributor. He's a tough nut who climbed his way to the top the hard way. He demands respect from his team, and while employees may not look at him as a friend, they know he gets results and they're happy to follow behind him.

David has confidence in his abilities, but the two entry level Gen Yers he recently hired are putting him to the test. Not only do they question every decision he makes, but they have the audacity to ask "why" when assigned a task. They have no interest in paying their dues and constantly ask for more challenging work. What's more, they're plugged into their iPods 24/7, check their Facebook accounts hourly, and show up dressed like they were out panhandling before coming to the office. They're getting their work done, but in David's opinion, they have no respect for the rules. He had to earn his way to the top and there's no way he's going to coddle these kids and hand them an easy ride.

But now let's slip into a pair Gen Y's shoes, which are probably flip flops, and walk a mile from their perspective. Both of David's new hires are excited about the job, but the boss sure can be a downer. He only sees the negative, and no matter how many questions they throw at him, he never seems to have any answers. It's not that he criticizes their work, but he sure rides them hard about the iPods, their clothes and the precious few minutes they spend social networking with their friends. If they have no problem skipping lunch or staying late when they have to, why can't they text a buddy once in a while to make some after work plans?

And what's the deal with all the grunt work? They're college grads with lots of skills. All this filing and data entry is okay, but how is it contributing to the big picture? When do they get to do something important? Just because they're the new guys, are they supposed to forget about honing their skills and furthering their careers? They both watched while their parents devoted a lifetime to an organization only to see them get shafted in company cut backs. So can you please explain to them the benefit of paying their dues?

It's David's command and control style of management and all his dated rules that are totally out of whack. And could he be anymore of a corporate clone? What's up with that tie he's always wearing? It's not like clients are waltzing through the office waiting to judge them on what they're wearing. If he's not going to blow his nose in it or use it as a napkin, what purpose does a tie really serve? Unless someone can tell them why closing up the neck hole of your shirt, especially when it's 100 degrees outside, makes you a more valuable employee, they're sticking with t shirts.

The natural impulse may be to tell Gen Y to suck it up and do what they're told, just like you did. But when you stop and consider the environment in which they were raised, you gain an understanding of why that won't fly. They're not like us; Gen Y's beliefs and values are worlds apart, and the old rules don't provide for a work environment that drives them to high performance. So if you look at the situation from the old way of doing things, yes; you're going to get angry and see Gen Y as nothing more than high maintenance.

Leaders that are truly invested in managing and motivating Gen Y keep their blood pressure in check by accepting that the younger generation is only expressing the social, political, and economic world in which they were raised. These leaders develop a base understanding of the world that shaped Gen Y so they can better meet their needs and expectations. And that includes Boomer generation leaders who, while they may have raised Gen Y kids, may not automatically see the truth about who they are and why.

We're not defending the foibles of Gen Y, or any other generation for that matter. And we're not suggesting you give them free reign to do whatever they want. Bridging the generation gap doesn't mean surrendering your own beliefs any more than it does forcing "them" to be more like "you." Bottom line, you don't have to agree with Gen Y, and you don't have to like their lifestyle. But you do need to find a way to tune in to them if you want to inspire high performance.

Peeling back the layers to see what makes Gen Y tick gives you a direct pipeline to their interests, motivations, aspirations and capabilities. And insider knowledge like that provides a real edge when it comes to managing these folks.

Gen Y Who Are They and Why?

*U*nlike the generations that came before them, Gen Y was born in to a child-centered universe that embraced a humanistic approach to parenting. There's conjecture that their Baby Boomer parents took things too far. That by crossing the line between caring and over-coddling, and exchanging discipline for doting, they left their kids critically unprepared for the real world. And some of that speculation comes from the Boomer parents themselves.

Whether or not you agree with Boomer parenting methods is inconsequential. But you can't erase 20 some odd years of influence. The early mirrors by which Gen Yers define themselves were established at birth and then nurtured over the years by parents, teachers and coaches. Leaders that think they can coerce Gen Y to conform to the old rules are wasting their time. Smart leaders learn to manage around the generational differences by developing an understanding of the world in which Gen Y was raised and how it shaped them into who they are today.

There are six major psychological elements that help explain why Gen Y acts and reacts the way they do:

1. Self esteem
2. Power
3. Technological authority
4. Immediacy
5. Customization
6. Concurrency

We're not implying these are the only factors that had a hand in creating the younger generation. At 70 million strong they're entering adulthood with countless unique experiences behind them. We encourage you to learn all you can to gain greater insight to these additional influences. But understanding these six core factors is all you need to create the foundation from which you can successfully manage and motive Gen Y.

Who They Are and Why Factor #1: Self Esteem

Gen Y's Baby Boomer parents invested time, energy and a good deal of money in making sure their kids knew they were unique, extraordinary, irreplaceable, and always deserving of reward. Bathed in self worth from the moment they were born, Gen Y was pampered, nurtured and programmed to believe they were truly something special. And the message not only came early; it came often and from multiple directions.

Dads, once content to pace outside the delivery room and pass out cigars, suddenly wanted bonding time with their newborns. Organizations responded by initiating paternity leave and some dads even assumed the full time role of Mr. Mom. But it wasn't just parents and the workplace that changed gears to accommodate and enforce the Gen Y prodigy. The consumer world took full advantage of the situation by launching an explosion of products that further propagated the belief that Gen Y babies weren't ordinary babies; they were special.

And it wasn't just pushchairs, strollers and buggies. Gen Y babies had infant computer software, subliminal programming CDs, cashmere diaper covers and electric warmers to lessen the jolt of cold baby wipes. Homes were elaborately childproofed and Gen Y babies were tucked securely "on board" complete with car seats and signage. And that first fall while learning to ride a bike was heavily cushioned by a helmet and elbow and knee pads. And if parents had any doubts that they weren't doing enough to enforce the message of "you're so special," Oprah showed them how to ask the source itself by introducing the world to baby whisperers.

Dr. Spock's long respected wisdom suddenly faced major competition as a new crop of child rearing experts commandeered bookstore shelves. Everyone had something to say, and Boomer parents were presented with options and a diverse selection of back up when the going got tough. But the one concept almost unanimously agreed upon was that good behavior should be rewarded and that it was entirely possible to love, nurture and support your child into compliance. Punishment was out and reward was in. If you made your kids feel good about the things they did right, they were bound to repeat the behavior.

The focus on self esteem only grew stronger as the kids matured. The average Gen Yer participated in multiple team sports, church activities, scouts, and music lessons to name just a few. And when it came to star performance, no one was disqualified. Excellence took a back seat to participation and effort, ensuring everyone who signed up got a trophy. As kids got older their proud parents replaced the Baby on Board signs with bumper stickers that boasted of honor roll children. And even when kids blatantly slacked off, parents went to bat to protect them from being labeled as anything less than the best. Like the mom in Massachusetts who petitioned (and won) public report of the school honor roll after one of her sons failed to make the grade.

Whether they were padded against falls, touted as the best, or sheltered from failure, Gen Y grew up largely protected from any feelings of negative self worth. They didn't learn the lesson that when you fall you get up, brush yourself off, and recoup your losses by trying harder the next time. Instead, Gen Y was raised to believe they were smarter than that; they didn't have to fall at all.

To those of us on the outside looking in, the younger generation appears to have an overwhelming sense of self worth and entitlement. But from Gen Y's perspective, they're simply demanding what they were repeatedly told is rightfully theirs.

Who They Are and Why Factor #2: Power

Encouraged to be both seen and heard, Gen Y questioned everything. In return, they were indulged by teachers, parents and coaches with the answers they were after. They never heard, "Pipe down, kid," or "Come back when I'm not so busy." They were special, and no matter what they had to say, the adults that mattered most were happy to hear them out.

Economically, Gen Y influenced their parents' spending patterns around factors such as where to vacation, what eat, where to live, and even what make and color car to buy. If Gen Y didn't like it, parents weren't buying it.

Advertisers recognized the power of this lucrative demographic and responded by branding and marketing directly to the kids. The communication was clear: we're listening and what you say counts.

Older generations may have had Saturday morning cartoons, but Gen Y had entire television stations programmed to play their favorites, 24 hours a day. And that alone leads the mind to wonder; I mean, what kid is watching TV at three in the morning? But for the few that were, it was right there waiting for them.

Gen Y grew up with all kinds of power. They're used to getting what they want, when they want it. And if one source fails to produce, they're accustomed to easily being able to find another that can. So when they walk into a workplace that's governed by the hierarchal system of the old rules, one that basically tells them to sit down and shut up until they earn the right, it's much like walking into a brick wall. Ironically, some mangers feel they're beating their heads into that same wall trying to bring Gen Y down a notch. The problem is Gen Y isn't going to relinquish the power they see as their birthright just because a boss enters the picture and tells them "No."

It's not that Gen Y doesn't respect authority; they've just been raised with a different understanding of what it means. Unlike older generations who couldn't wait to get out from under parental control, Gen Y has always depended heavily on parents and other adults to answer their questions and help guide them through life. They grew up seeing adults as friends, and that's changed the rules on what constitutes respect. They've been a part of the adult world nearly all their lives, and parents, teachers and coaches have always been there to help, nurture and support; not to tell them they couldn't do something.

Who They Are and Why Factor # 3: Technological Authority

Twenty years ago a new employee wasn't better than the boss at anything. Folks came into an organization green and were happy to start at the bottom and see how far they could go. But that's no longer true. Gen Y is the first generation that can truly point to something where they are smarter than their elders: technology. And walking into the workplace with the knowledge that you're more skilled than the guy running the company definitely imposes some changes to traditional organizational structures, at least from Gen Y's point of view.

It's not just the ease with which Gen Y uses technology that instills such confidence; it's also how they make the most of it. Technology is where the younger generation goes to solve problems, find answers and keep in touch. They think nothing of simultaneously IMing friends while updating their blog and downloading tunes to their iPod. All of which they do with amazing speed.

The older generations often look down at text talk and accuse Gen Y of lacking in written skills. After all, it's certainly not proper English. But is short hand, a skill that not long ago was a bargaining chip for the best secretaries, really superior to texting? Gen Y may be focused on a different set of P's and Q's than their older generation co-workers, but most of them have a real knack for finding new and better ways to use technology. And in an ever changing and rapidly moving world, that's a real advantage. As the Gen Y creators of social networking sites like Facebook and MySpace can attest, technological savvy brings the big rewards in today's world.

We may be bragging when we say that our five year old is more adept on a computer than we are, but that fact hasn't been lost on Gen Y. When it comes to technology, they're used to having adults turn to them for advice and help. And when they fix our unfixable problems with just a few clicks, they're used to being told how amazing they are. Gen Y's "I can do it all" attitude may be irritating to a lot of managers, but it's easy to see how that sense of unprecedented confidence was born.

Gen Y's technical know how leaves managers that are accustomed to shaping employees from the ground up facing a new challenge. Not only are egos on both sides put to task, but one of the greatest dangers of Gen Y's sense of confidence is that it blindsides them to the soft skill aspects of the job in which they do need additional training. And that's a reality that Gen Y may not be readily willing to accept. Remember, this is a generation that's used to having their strengths celebrated and their weaknesses downplayed.

Who They Are and Why Factor # 4: Immediacy

Remember saving box tops to get a prize? It could take weeks or even months to collect enough, and then you still had to wait another six or eight weeks for the fruit of your labors to arrive. Try telling that to Gen Y and I guarantee they'll think you're pulling their leg. That's because the last time they had to wait that long for anything was when they were in-utero, waiting to be born.

For the oldest members of Gen Y, life before immediate gratification is a foggy memory at best, and for the youngest, it's the stuff of mythology. Whenever they needed knowledge, it was right at their fingertips, and overnight delivery was the norm, not a luxury. Gen Y not only is used to getting stuff fast, they're also used to moving fast. They make quick decisions, want instant action, expect immediate results, and think for the short-term.

When you start to analyze your processes against the speed at which Gen Y lives life, it becomes clear that many of the traditional approaches to business take as long to deliver a reward as your box top prize took to land in the mailbox. And that typically doesn't sit well with a generation for whom speed, not patience, is a virtue. Whether you like it or not, they're going to press you to move faster and to upgrade and change the way you do things.

If you resist and make them wait too long to see results, even if they're only 23, they'll tell you that they feel like they're wasting their life in a dead end job. Or they might say nothing at all and simply leave, in search of a workplace that makes an effort to keep up with them.

Who They Are and Why Factor # 5: Customization

Gen Y is used to being able to bend the rules to their will. From home pages to web pages, right down to the car they drive, customization is what this generation is all about. Even utilitarian devices like iPods and cell phones represent a form of self expression through custom skins, ring tones, and a slew of other features. They don't remember a world of mass production where you took what you could get; they've always been able to get it the way they want. And as the consumer world quickly learned, if you want Gen Y's interest and loyalty, you've got to offer them options for personalization.

Gen Y's love of customization carries right over to the workplace. You can design a job to encompass activities A thru Z, but that doesn't mean Gen Y is going to automatically accept what you hand them. They may want to do half the tasks on your job description and share the others with coworkers.

Or they may want to delete some tasks entirely and add in others. Incentive, reward and recognition programs are also prime targets for customization. And if you're thinking of just saying no, think again. This is Generation 'Why', and they're going to want to know, why not? And saying, "Because that's the way we do things around here," just isn't going to cut it.

Who They Are and Why Factor # 6: Concurrency

Gen Y has always done it all. Their schedule has never been short of activities, and whether it was on the soccer field or in the classroom, their efforts were held in high esteem. Boomer parents were invested in making sure their kids didn't miss a single opportunity, and now that Gen Y is thinking for themselves, not much has changed. They still want it all, and since they lack the critical insight that you can't really do everything well, it's not easy to get Gen Y to make some choices about what they really do want.

Part of the problem is that they watched their parents slowly creep up the professional ladder of success only to witness them get pushed off with little to show for a huge sacrifice of time and dedication. Gen Y isn't about to make the same mistake. They're in control of their destiny, and climbing to the top one rung at a time just isn't an option. They don't want an either/or choice; they want it all, and they want it in a hurry. They've been told they're special, talented and worthy since birth; so what's the hold up?

Leaders tend to feel challenged, and in some cases intimidated, by Gen Y's eagerness to have it all. The old rules presented a system of dues that needed to be paid before you get ahead. And when you've climbed to the top via the school of hard knocks, it's easy to get irritated by anyone who suddenly decides to change the status quo and make things easier.

But Gen Y has never been taught to play that game. They've been padded and protected since birth, and they see no value in learning the hard way. It's second nature for Gen Y to find the least difficult route and to make up their own rules as they go along. And they've never been told to do it any other way. For the younger generation, this approach has redefined not just how they play the game, but also what it means to win.

If you want to know what made your Gen Y employees the way they are, it isn't hard to find out. They're pretty eager to share; just go to one of their blogs or MySpace accounts and you'll see their willingness to let it all hang out. Smart leaders take advantage of Gen Y's transparency. They read between the lines and separate the unrealistic expectations common to youth of any generation from the factors that warrant workplace change. They reach out to Gen Y with words and actions they can understand instead of alienating them with a stubborn and unrealistic demand to conform.

When you set the new rules into motion everyone wins. You help Gen Y employees find the professional happiness they seek and provide your organization with productive and tech-savvy team members. And as an added bonus, you'll likely find that many of your older generation employees; once they get used to the changes, are happy to see the old rules disappear.

NEW RULE #1:

Gen Y Needs Real-Time Positive Reinforcement to Measure Success

Gen Y employees are entering the workforce with twenty-odd years of life experience that doesn't come close to preparing them for the real world. But that doesn't make them less valuable. They just need strong leadership to push them to the top of their capabilities. But the old rule of negative reinforcement to get results isn't going to work on a generation that has always measured performance success based on positive feedback.

Employer approval is the number one predictor of Gen Y job satisfaction. Yet, according to a Leadership IQ survey, only 39 percent of the younger generation said their boss does a good job of recognizing and acknowledging their accomplishments. That's six out of every ten Gen Y employees that aren't getting the one thing they want most. It's also a lot of employees that may be underperforming because they have no idea what high performance looks like, and whether or not they're delivering it.

A lot of leaders are reluctant to put much stock in positive reinforcement. It seems too much like praise. And while Gen Y's parents may have been eager to dole it out by the bucket load, it's not going to happen at work. The thought process is that you're hired to do the job and if you do it right you keep getting paid. What more reward or reinforcement do you need?

But we're not talking about handing out fluffy compliments just for sake of making someone feel good. Nor do we believe that delivering undeserved reward with meaningless trophies is the way to manage Gen Y. The day your Gen Y employee walks through your doors marks the end of the parent/child relationship and initiates a new boss/employee interaction. You're not the only one for whom the rules are changing. Gen Y has plenty to learn, but unless you reach out to them on a level they can understand, your leadership and direction will fall on deaf ears.

Positive reinforcement isn't praise. It's a teaching tool that addresses the well documented psychological principle that says desirable behavior when reinforced tends be repeated. On the flip side, negative reinforcement, while it can work to cease unwanted behavior, does nothing to optimize performance. As anyone who has been on the receiving end of negative reinforcement knows, the motivation is to figure out what not to do as quickly as possible in order to wipe out the punishment. But when you communicate a clear message that says, "The thing you just did right there; that way...it's good. Do more of it," you deliver feedback that increases the frequency and intensity of the behavior you want.

The Four Components of Positive Reinforcement

There are four ruling factors by which leaders need to abide when giving positive reinforcement:

- Make it meaningful
- Be specific
- Catch them in the act
- Don't cloud the message with criticism

Make It Meaningful

You don't need to blow constant smoke to keep Gen Y motivated. In fact, doling out meaningless praise is guaranteed to work against you. That world in which Gen Y grew up where everyone got a trophy just for showing up had an impact on the middle and high performers. They hate it when everyone gets the same reward. It provides no learning curve and no differentiation that their performance stands out from everyone else's. It's not exactly a statement of higher intelligence, nor much of an honor, to make the dean's list when everyone else does too. The only folks that appreciate empty praise are low performers.

One leader found this out the hard way. When Tom brought on his first Gen Y employee he was far from oblivious to the management challenges it presented. He had a niece that was Gen Y, and he'd seen first hand the culture of praise in which she'd been raised. He was determined to do things right by his Gen Yer, and he knew that his old style of managing by negative reinforcement wasn't going to cut it.

The company was in the middle of a massive mailing that due to budget cuts was being done in house. Tom set his new employee, Madison, to work stuffing envelopes. Anxious to enforce the level of high performance expected from employees, Tom called Madison in to his office at the end of the first week for a casual chat. *"I'm really impressed with your work,"* he told her. *"Your envelope stuffing skills are really terrific."* Then he sat back and waited for a sign that the positive reinforcement had registered.

"You're kidding, right?" was Madison's response.

When Tom pushed for an explanation to her reaction, Madison said that his comment was a total insult. She didn't mind stuffing envelopes; it was part of the job. But to imply that her performance on a menial task was something special, especially when she had so much more to offer, was belittling. Tom learned two lessons that day. The first was that empty praise holds no value with Gen Y. Complimenting employees for unchallenging tasks, or work they didn't actually do, is counterproductive and only diminishes their trust. The second was that Madison, true to her generation, wasn't afraid to speak her mind.

Be Specific

Another manager, Daniel, was a great believer in the power of praise. He made it a point to circulate the office once a day and compliment his employees on the good work he saw taking place. As he made the rounds he would spurt out statements like, *"Looking good,"* *"Keep up the hard work,"* and *"That's what I like to see."* Despite his good intentions, Daniel's words were too vague to deliver any message of value. The only thing he inspired from his team was some snickering at his predicable words.

"Great job" doesn't qualify as positive reinforcement. It's empty praise and it delivers a zero learning curve. Which means the employee on the receiving end will probably take it in one ear and send it out the other. In order to be effective, positive reinforcement must provide a clear picture of the specific performance that's being commended. And when we say specific, we mean specific. Otherwise employees will have no clue what behavior you want to see again.

It may seem as if the generic *"great job"* comment goes up a notch if you tack on something like, *"I like your attention to detail."* But that still doesn't specify what details you actually like. Since Gen Yers typically are very visual learners, one technique is to paint a picture with your words that exactly describes the behavior you are commending. Because the more clearly employees understand the behavior you want, the more you leverage the way they appraise their own performance. And that delivers a double whammy as the positive reinforcement is first heard and then processed internally.

When Daniel started changing the rules, the first thing he addressed was the way he delivered positive reinforcement. Instead of just circling the office and throwing out random comments, he made a point to come to a full stop in front of the employee he wished to address. Once he had the employee's attention he would say something like, *"Aaron, the way you got this report done ahead of schedule means a lot to both me and the customer. Given the short deadline, I'm especially pleased to see there are no typos. It's obvious you spent considerable time proofreading it. Oh, and the extra data analyses are really creative."*

You can be sure there wasn't any employee snickering that day. Most folks were left wondering what they could do to win similar positive attention from the boss. As for Aaron, he had a lot to think about: *"You know; I did do a good job on that report. I had to put in some overtime to get it done early, but it sure was worth it. It felt really good to have Daniel take notice of my efforts like that. I wasn't sure about the extra data analyses, but I guess it's a good idea. I'll make sure to do that and the proofreading again next time. You know, I might even have some ideas to make next month's report even better. How cool would it be if I could get Daniel to tell me I topped this month's performance?"*

When positive reinforcement provides a visualization of the specific skills and abilities that constitute desirable high performance, employees have something to grab onto and run with. It delivers a message that registers with Gen Y as a positive measurement of success. And feeling good is a high that most folks want to replicate. Consequently, employees are going to reflect on the performance that earned them that good feeling in an effort to reproduce or even surpass it.

Catch Them in the Act

Positive reinforcement depends on a brain connection that associates the reward with the desired behavior. And for a generation that grew up with a constant flow of positive feedback, yearly or quarterly reviews aren't going to do the trick. Asking them to wait a year for some constructive feedback is like asking them to wait an eternity. In order to have any effect, positive reinforcement has to be delivered in real time.

Remember, Gen Y grew up on information overload. Whether they were after knowledge or just casual input from friends, all they had to do was text or Google to get an immediate response. They probably won't bother to stick around and wait for a yearly message, and if they do, it's bound to have little to no meaning. So when you see Gen Y doing something you like, let them know about it right there and then.

Look for the teachable moments and give supportive documentation as they're happening. When Aaron handed in the report early, Daniel was right there to say, *"Hey. You got this done ahead of schedule and that's terrific. I love it and our client is going to love it too."* Think about the impact of that message six, eight or twelve months after the fact. If the boss even remembered to include it in a yearly review, it would likely leave Aaron scratching his head and wondering, *"What report?"*

Don't Cloud the Message with Criticism

There's a place and a time for constructive criticism, but it isn't when you're delivering a positive message. Don't make the mistake of trying to squeeze a negative performance critique or correction between layers of positive reinforcement. At Leadership IQ we call it the Compliment Sandwich, and it doesn't work.

Joanne was having trouble motivating one of her Gen Y employees to adhere to company policy regarding customer service. She had just started using positive reinforcement with her staff and had already seen some results. So she figured if she laced some criticism in with the positive stimuli she could essentially kill two birds and still come off looking like the good guy.

She pulled her employee aside and said, *"Ashley, I wanted to tell you what a great job you did dealing with that difficult customer last week. Even though she was visibly upset you kept your cool and helped her resolve the problem. Satisfied customers are what we are here to create. I did notice you arguing with another customer this afternoon though, and that isn't so good. But again, last week, you were right on target."*

Ashley returned to the selling floor and Joanne was hopeful that her message had been received. Her goal had been to soften the blow of the criticism with the good feeling that comes with positive reinforcement, but to still let Ashley know she needed to improve. Ashley's coworkers were on her in an instant, curious about what had just gone down with the boss. *"Oh, it was nothing bad,"* Ashley told them. *"Remember that crazy customer I had last week? I guess Joanne is happy I didn't flip out on her or anything. I don't know. I'm not really sure what she wanted. I guess she was just trying to be nice."*

Joanne struck out on both counts by using a Compliment Sandwich. Her positive message was received, but it was clouded by the negative feedback layered in the middle. As for the constructive criticism, it wasn't heard at all. If anything, Ashley got a slight boost that her performance was good, but the negative behavior remained untouched.

Positive reinforcement is about being in the moment with something that was done right. Don't waste the opportunity by trying to turn it into a buffer for bad news. If you have to deliver corrections or criticisms, keep it for another time. And make sure that when the employee responds to the criticism and delivers the desirable behavior that you let them know, right way and in detail, what they did right.

Gen Y Has Two Modes of Communication: Good and Bad

Past generations of employees could go days without talking to the boss and not think twice about it. Silence was golden, and if nothing was being said it was safe to assume that all was well. Likewise, friendships were able to survive for months at a time with little or no communication. But to Gen Y, who grew up in a high-tech world that encouraged a constant exchange of messaging, no news is bad news and silence equals disapproval.

One need only look at the number of text messages (often up to 200 a day) the average Gen Yer sends to recognize the speed and repetitiveness with which this generation regularly touches base. They rely on constant feedback to stay focused and engaged. If they're not tagging one another on Facebook, or tweeting on Twitter, they're texting cryptic bites of information that detail their every move. Leaders that respond to this by giving their Gen Yers the frequent feedback they crave will build employee confidence about the things they're doing right and correct performance problems before they get out of hand.

Lucy noticed an immediate change in the performance level of her Gen Y employees when she started to give more frequent feedback. At first, it seemed like an inconvenience that would require additional time, a luxury her work day didn't allow. But she quickly found how little time it actually took to hone in on positive behavior and reward it with informal recognition.

She found there was substantial performance payback from a statement as simple as, *"Joe, I've noticed you coming in early and staying late while we've been trying to close the Hellmann account. The client is thrilled and it's exactly the kind of high performance I'm looking for."* And the day she sent her first group text message to thank her employees for a job well done, the response from her Gen Yers was tremendous:

I **realy aprec8 d xtra ef4T** on **d** Smith **acct**. **d xtra hrs, add'tl rsrch n** team collaboration **ErnD** us a **nu n** profitable client. I **TY 1 n ll**.

Lucy had to use an online translator to figure out the lingo, and she doubted she would ever replace face-to-face feedback on important issues with techno talk. But making the effort to reach out to her Gen Yers in their own language went a long way to bridge the cultural disconnect.

Performance Appraisals

We know that frequent positive reinforcement is critical to helping Gen Y achieve their personal best. However, the reality is that even though most employees hate performance appraisals, and despite the fact that they produce minimal results, many organizations still enforce a policy of periodic formal review. If you find yourself in a position where you're forced to comply, you can still take some steps to make sure the experience results in a positive outcome.

We did a survey that showed only 14% of employees felt their performance appraisal provided meaningful and relevant feedback. And that's not doing a lot to give Gen Y the positive reinforcement they want. But it's easy to turn that around, and as an added bonus, you'll extract some valuable performance information.

Nothing ticks Gen Y off as much as when they do positive stuff and don't get noticed for it. So before you go into the performance appraisal, have employees give you a list of their proudest moments. This will ensure you don't miss the high-touch opportunity to reward these important moments.

That same list will also tell you quite a bit about the kind of performer you have. If an employee sets his or her expectations low and tells you they're proud they made it to work 80 percent of the time, that tells you something about where this review is going to go. On the flip side, if you've got someone that's got a list of worthy accomplishments, you may gain awareness of factors you didn't even know about. And that provides you with the opportunity to recognize and reward meritorious behavior.

Putting It Together

Janice is the executive director of a senior living community. She worked her way up the company ladder over the last two decades and loves both the organization and her job. While Janice commands the respect of her staff and is generally well liked, she still worries that being a woman gives subordinates the impression that she's a pushover. Consequently, she's pretty stingy when it comes to giving out praise. Her current staff includes three new administrative hires, the first Gen Y employees Janice has managed.

Janice grew up in a household where her father's word was law, and if you defied it, the punishment was harsh. She attributes her strong work ethic to her upbringing and expects the same from her staff. When performance is under par, she generally uses the same negative reinforcement techniques she grew up with to generate results. And it's always been effective. That is, until the Gen Yers joined the team. Janice sees potential in each of her three new employees, but she's finding it difficult to reach them in a leadership capacity. They just don't seem to respond in the same way as do the older generations.

The Gen Y employees, April, Parker and Trent, are all recent college grads. They each came to the job for different reasons. April has an interest in pursuing geriatric medicine; Parker wants to join the Peace Corps and hopes the experience gives him an edge; and Trent is currently without any real direction. His mom knows Janice from college and she pulled some strings to get him the job.

Despite their different directions, April, Parker and Trent share the same confusion when it comes to their new boss. They agree that Janice is smart, but she doesn't provide them with any real direction to follow. They've discussed amongst themselves quitting in order look for better jobs, and April is getting close to giving her notice.

Workplace grapevines being what they are, Janice quickly caught wind that her youngest employees were unhappy. As much as it pained her to admit it, she realized she was going to have to make some changes in her management style if she wanted to retain her new hires. They were good kids with great skill sets, and she had neither the time nor the resources to conduct another hiring campaign. Besides, she knew the problems she was facing would be the same with anyone that fell into the Gen Y age bracket.

Giving up her command and control leadership style that left little to no room for positive reinforcement was quite a stretch. But Janice was determined. She decided to take it a step at a time and see how it went.

Trent was having the greatest performance difficulties, so she started by directing her focus on him.

Trent was working on setting up a calendar of weekly resident outings to places like art galleries, museums and the theatre. Despite working on the project for over a week, the calendar remained empty. Janice had been considering turning the job over to Parker, and had mentioned as much to Trent. She hoped the threat of losing a fun work assignment would give him some incentive to kick it into gear, but it hadn't worked.

She pulled Trent aside and asked him how the job was progressing. It was like someone had had let the air out of him. Trent's whole body physically deflated and his energy just seemed to vanish. But his mind was racing with the following thoughts: Janice had already laid into him twice this week about the stupid calendar. He had like a hundred calls out; it wasn't his fault nobody was returning them. He was tired of talking about it. Janice had nothing good to say to him; it was like she was out to get him. He wondered what his mom was thinking when she made him take the job.

Janice couldn't tell what Trent was thinking, but his silence and body language indicated it wasn't anything good. She jumped right in with the statement she had rehearsed the night before. *"I was just looking at your call log. I'm very impressed with the creative thought you've given to this project. We've never had a program coordinator who thought of outings like foreign films and classes at the meditation center. I also see you're trying to swing us into the Degas exhibition at the museum next month. I think our residents will appreciate it; they're always excited about new experiences."*

Trent was pleasantly shocked to have Janice speak to him on this level. He actually was enjoying his work on the calendar; he was just frustrated that he couldn't get any results. For the first time he felt like he could trust Janice and ask her for help. It didn't seem like she was going to yell at him. *"Yeah, I'm pretty excited about those things too,* Trent said. *" I actually have a buddy from college who works at the museum and is trying to get us our own tour guide. I'm just not really hearing back from anyone with a definite. What do you suggest I do?"*

Janice couldn't be happier. It was the first time any of her three Gen Yers had asked for her advice. She and Trent explored some of the ways he could secure dates with his contacts, and he eagerly returned to his desk to get to work.

Later that day she noticed April reviewing the monthly invoices. This was a sore spot around the residence as invoices always had mistakes and went out late. Janice had made it clear when she delegated this task to April that she wanted it done on time, and miracle of miracles, here she was doing as asked.

Janice jumped right on this opportunity for positive reinforcement. *"April, I can't tell you how thrilled I am that you're reviewing the invoices on schedule. I know you've got other projects going on, and I'm impressed with your ability to schedule yourself so everything gets done. The residents are going to be really happy to get these on time and without error. This goes a long way towards making our organization more professional."*

The genuine smile Janice got in response from April told her plenty. Lately it had seemed as if April was never happy. She buried her head in her work and then scurried out at the end of the day. Her performance was fine, but her passion had definitely been lacking. Janice could see already that a single hit of positive reinforcement had effected a change in April's attitude.

Since things were going so well, Janice decided to seek out Parker and try the new rule with him. Parker was inputting into Excel the information she'd given him for next week's schedule. The technical competence all three of the Gen Yers brought to the job was a relief for Janice. She'd had to teach older generation employees Excel more times than she cared to remember, and they always got tangled up in some problem with it. *"Parker, it's so nice to know I can rely on you to do the schedule,"* she said. *"I really appreciate your ability with Excel."*

Parker looked up from his work in disbelief. Janice immediately recognized her error. There was no way Parker was going to take her comment as it was intended. To him, the Excel task was rudimentary work that he was basically stuck with because no one else knew how to do it. If anything, her statement was an insult to his intelligence. She immediately confessed her error by saying, *"I don't mean to imply that Excel is the only thing that gives you value around here. I really just wanted you to know that you're doing a good job."*

As the words came out, Janice realized she'd blundered again. She'd offered no specific reference to what Parker did that made him so valuable. But then she noticed him smiling, and when he said, *"Thanks, Janice. I really do appreciate the compliment,"* she knew there was an opportunity for another chance. She'd wait for a genuine teachable moment and try again.

All in all, Janice felt her first stab at the new rule had gone amazingly well. The gap between the generations wasn't exactly closed, but she had finally found a way to reach out to her Gen Yers so they heard and responded to her. What's more, she'd learned that it was okay to mess up. The very fact that she was trying to give her Gen Y employees a little more of what they wanted made a difference. She was even thinking of trying some positive reinforcement with her older generation employees. Not only did it seem to work, but it felt nice to not always be the bad guy.

NEW RULE #2:

Constructive Criticism is a Two-Way Communication

*P*ositive reinforcement will go far towards creating a culture of high-performance. However, there will still be times when you need to negatively critique a Gen Y employee's performance in order to effect a necessary change. But because Gen Yers were brought up on a steady diet of praise, relying on the old-rule method of delivering constructive criticism is guaranteed to backfire.

Under the old rule, leaders typically delivered critical feedback with a blunt analysis of the undesirable behavior. If they wanted something changed, they made a statement like: "Tim, your organizational skills are terrible; do something about it." And for the most part, this direct approach to criticism worked.

Older generation employees may have harbored feelings of hurt, anger and defensiveness at getting dressed down by the boss, but if they valued their jobs, they kept quiet and made the necessary changes. Over time, some leaders tempered the delivery with tweaks to make the criticism sound kinder and gentler. Addendums to the rule such as, "criticize the action, not the person," and "layer the criticism with praise," became commonplace. But for the most part, the process remained a one-way conversation.

As we saw in New Rule #1, the old-rule elements of fear and intimidation aren't going to awaken a commitment to change in Gen Y. We know their early development by positive reinforcement provided them with a thinner skin than their older generation peers. That means that even the "nice" version of old-rule criticism will drastically shrink their self esteem. The feelings of inferiority, worthlessness, and mistrust a poorly presented criticism inspires will likely cause Gen Y to send up their Walls of Defensiveness. And once those invisible strong holds are in place, your message doesn't stand a chance at being heard.

The new rule takes a softer approach to delivering constructive criticism. It promotes positive growth in Gen Y employees without targeting their delicate sense of self esteem. The following techniques will allow you to tell your younger generation employees that they need to improve while still bolstering morale with a positive 'can do' attitude.

I.D.E.A.L.S for Delivering Constructive Criticism

There are six steps for delivering constructive criticism that will ensure Gen Y positively hears and processes the correction:

- I: Invite them to partner
- D: Disarm yourself
- E: Eliminate blame
- A: Affirm their control
- L: List correct feedback
- S: Synchronize your understanding

When applied collectively, these techniques generate a domino effect that knocks down, and keeps down, the Walls of Defensiveness. Let's take a look at how I.D.E.A.L.S. works to keep Gen Y employees feeling safe, open, and receptive to critical feedback.

Invite Them to Partner

Gen Y doesn't have the same fear of authority as older generation employees. They're also not accustomed to sitting in silence while being spoken to by someone in a position of authority. Boomer parents treated their kids almost as equals. They allowed them an active role in communication and gave their opinions considerable weight. An invitation to partner in dialog signals to Gen Y that while the boss may have a problem with them, the meeting isn't going to be a bash session. And entering into a congenial interchange, even if they have done something wrong, will make Gen Yers feel safe to talk about the situation.

Even if you already know the end result you want, you still need to make your Gen Y employees feel secure that you're open to hearing their side. One leader, Katy, was forced to talk to a Gen Y employee, Jill, who was continually ignoring the company dress code. Jill had been given adequate warning and Katy was fed up with her behavior. If she had her way, Katy would have liked to have said, "I want to talk about why you refuse to listen to my direction and continue to be defiant. I don't want to hear any excuses; I just want it to stop." Of course, this sort of old rule approach would only succeed in making Jill feel defensive. And Katy knew that once Jill's Walls of Defensiveness went up, there would be no chance of solving the problem.

Katy wanted Jill to hear and understand what she was saying in a way that motivated an adjustment in behavior. So she went with a positive approach and asked Jill if she would partner in dialog. Katy's invite was simple: "Jill, would you be willing to have a talk about company policy regarding employee dress code?" The invite made it clear that the meeting wasn't going to be praise session. However, Jill felt secure from Katy's calm tone and invitation to talk it wasn't going to be a yelling session either. It even seemed like she would have a chance to state her side of the story.

Face-to-face is always preferable when inviting an employee to partner in dialog. Not only do the words convey a non-confrontational situation, but when folks hear a relaxed tone and see friendly body language, it enhances their receptivity to the invitation. In some cases, if the pre-existing relationship is strong enough, you can send your invite via email or even text. Gen Y loves getting text messages from the boss; it shows an effort to communicate using their preferred language. However you extend the invite, the main thing is to erase all signs of intimidation or fear from your words. You want to send a clear message that this is just two people sitting down to exchange information and come to a resolution.

It's always a good idea to provide some options as to when the talk will take place. People naturally feel safer and perform better when they have choices. This is as easy as following up your invite with a statement like, "Do you want to talk now, or would you prefer to wait until after lunch?" While, in theory, you are offering them a choice, the catch is that you wrote the options based upon what you need and want.

There is one caveat to the invitation to partner technique. If you have a notoriously poor or confrontational relationship with the employee in question, and there's a very real possibility he or she will respond, "No, I'm not willing to have a conversation with you," an invite won't work. In this case, you want to turn your invite into a statement such as, "We need to have a conversation about company dress code." But be very careful here. You should forgo the invitation format only when a negative relationship exists. Otherwise, you risk seriously damaging a neutral or positive relationship.

Disarm Yourself

Until your Gen Yers feel confident that you've eliminated hurtful criticism from your arsenal of communication, they're likely to enter the conversation with some trepidation. And that can thwart your message from being heard. This is especially important if you've already established yourself as a leader who relies on the old rules. You want to openly disarm yourself so employees feel safe that no weapons of communication will be used.

Christian is a department manager with 25 direct reports, most of them Gen Y. They're a good team and he tries to be a fair boss, but the unyielding pressure from his own superior often makes Christian hot headed and emotional. Word got out that some of Christian's team was using company time and computers to send emails, update Facebook accounts, and conduct other personal business. Christian was given an ultimatum to either change the behavior or change jobs.

He went back to his department and called an emergency meeting. As his team piled in they noticed Christian's face was beet red. His mouth was turned down in an ugly scowl and his arms were crossed against his chest. "Here it comes again," they all thought, "Another verbal beating."

And they were right. Christian launched into his attack by basically repeating the same old-rule approach his own boss had used: "You guys are making me look bad again and I'm sick and tired of it. We're either gonna make some changes in attitude around here or we're gonna make some changes in staff." The Walls of Defensiveness shot up in every direction, blocking out everything else Christian said.

The situation would have played out differently if Christian had openly disarmed himself in front of his employees. First, he should have taken some time to cool off after being dressed down by his boss. Then he could have tried a tactic like personally approaching individual or small groups of team members and saying, "There have been some complaints about employees using the Internet for personal use during work hours. Would you be willing to meet as a group and figure out how we can solve this problem? I want everyone to work together to find a comfortable resolve, so I encourage you to bring along any ideas you may have."

By enforcing the fact that he was open to hearing their side of the story, Christian affirmed that this would be a reciprocal conversation. His Gen Y employees, who were used to taking a beating, would certainly take note of the change in his approach. And because Christian personally delivered the invitation in a calm and rational manner, it went the extra mile to show this wouldn't be another anger session that was filled with blame and accusations.

Judgment is another verbal weapon that can stand in the way of an effective critique. It quickly turns a conversation from constructive to destructive, and will make Gen Yers feel incompetent and discouraged. Publicly disarming yourself of judgment can be as simple as halting the flow of conversation from time to time by saying, "I'd like to review the situation to make sure I'm on the same page as you."

If you discover you're on different wavelengths, you'll need to backtrack and correct the situation. Taking this extra step doesn't mean you're going to necessarily agree with the other party, but it does send a reassuring message that you want to non-judgmentally understand a perspective other than your own.

When a disconnect occurs, make sure you don't bring judgment into situation with statements like:

- "You're not making any sense."
- You're not listening to me."

or it's shorter cousin:

- "Listen to me."

While "You're not making any sense" may sound innocuous enough at first, it actually points the "You" finger of blame. It implies the other person lacks knowledge and understanding, and says, "You're incapable of presenting a clear argument." And the same goes for "You're not listening." And for Gen Yers, who are used to having their opinions heard and respected, nothing will shut them down faster.

Instead of saying, "You're not listening to me," assume personal responsibility for the disconnect by saying, "I don't think I'm doing a good job of explaining myself." And instead of "You're not making any sense," try, "Could you help me understand this issue?" These simple rewrites erase the accusations and keep the conversation open and fluid. After all, does it really matter who's to blame and why? Isn't the more important issue getting the employee to hear what needs to be said so they execute a change?

Eliminate Blame

Even if you don't share the same perspective on a situation as your Gen Y employee, you can still work together to develop a plan that moves in a positive direction. The goal is to avoid historical and emotional punishment and focus on solutions. You don't want to make the other party feel bad for whatever they may have done or thought.

Reassure your partner in dialog that you have no intention of playing the blame game. You can say something right in your invite like, "If we find we have different perspectives we can discuss that and develop a plan for moving forward." Or, if you're in the middle of the conversation and see that a difference of opinion exists, interject by saying, "I see we have very different opinions on this. That's fine. But let's work together to find a resolve."

Affirm Their Control

In order to keep Gen Y employees fully engaged in the conversation, it's important to reaffirm that they have some control over the situation. Check in on a regular basis by saying something like, "Does that sound OK?", "Do you have any questions?" or "What are your thoughts?" This reminds them that they have a say in the matter and that you care about how they are doing and what they are thinking.

When you check in to affirm control, it's also a quick litmus test of whether the other party remains receptive to your words. If the answer is, "No, that doesn't sound okay to me," or you get a rapid-fire list of defensive questions in response, you can be pretty sure the conversation is off track. Again, you need to back pedal and fix this situation before you move on.

List Correct Feedback

The most successful leaders take nothing for granted when they deliver constructive criticism. It's not that they doubt Gen Y's intelligence or feel the need to hyper manage. They simply recognize that the younger generation is used to being able to customize things to their own specifications. And because they grew up being rewarded for participation and effort rather than performance, it doesn't hurt to take the extra effort to make a crystal clear statement that details exact expectations.

The golden rule for giving constructive feedback is:
- Makes perfect sense
- Holds up to logical scrutiny
- Is understandable
- Teaches sufficiently

The following two techniques will make sure you hit every factor of the golden rule.

Don't Skimp on the Details

No matter how small a detail may be, if it's something employees are going to be held accountable for, make sure you give them the information they need. A lot of leaders worry that giving hyper critical feedback makes them come off like a control freak or a micro manager. Admirably, they take conscious steps to temper their words and refrain from harping on the intimate details of how they want something done.

Granted, no one wants to work under a micro manager. And certainly, employees that feel they have the trust and confidence of the boss more often than not remain happily engaged in their work. But when clarity is sacrificed as part of the preventative, no one wins.

There's a simple rule that establishes the dividing line between what constitutes micro managing and constructive criticism:

If something is NOT optional, and you WILL hold the subordinate accountable if they don't do it, you MUST give clear and logical feedback.

Nothing kills employee morale faster than when the boss withholds critical information and then admonishes employees when results fail to meet expectations. This happens in countless cases where the boss doesn't even realize he or she has failed to provide clear directions. Protect yourself and your employees from this situation by never assuming there is a thorough understanding of anything for which employees can be punished or fired.

When Joan hired her first Gen Yer, she was determined to stick to the old rules. Coddling wasn't her style. Employees could either make the effort to be part of the team and meet organizational expectations, or they were welcome to leave. So when Blake, her new hire, showed up the first day wearing a logo t-shirt and flip flops, she pulled him aside and said, *"In this organization we dress appropriately. I suggest you take another look at the employee handbook regarding company dress code."*

Blake walked away from the interaction confused. He even stopped by the restroom to check himself out in the mirror. His hair was combed and his clothes were clean and unwrinkled; that seemed appropriate to him. He figured Joan must be having a pretty bad time of it if she was railing into him on his first day. He vaguely remembered being handed some literature when he was in HR, but he wasn't a big reader. He texted, and he talked, but things like handbooks or even emails weren't for him.

Joan's criticism provides too many possible interpretations, especially to a Gen Yer who's used to bending the rules. The same goes for criticisms like, *"We treat customers in a courteous manner,"* or *"We maintain the highest standards of professionalism."* The only way to ensure that employees meet and surpass expectations is by giving constructive feedback that includes specific behavioral standards.

No doubt Joan would have generated positive results if she had instead said something like, *"Blake, due to safety regulations, flip flops are never allowed in this workplace. Plain t-shirts with no logos are okay, but if you are meeting with a client, or we have outside people in the office, we want to present a more formal presence. That means a dress shirt and slacks---not jeans--- only. In these situations, I always send out a reminder email the day before. Maybe you'd like to receive this communication by text instead?"*

Explain Why

Past generations of employees may have been happy to do anything or go anywhere the leader wanted with no questions asked. But not Gen Y. True to their nickname of Gen Why?, they want to know *why* they're being asked to do something. This is the aspect of giving constructive criticism that most managers miss, and it's often the factor that makes or breaks what Gen Y does, how well it's done, and how happy they are doing it. When there's a link between what they're doing and the overall goal, you get improved performance.

If you tell your Gen Yers they can't wear t-shirts with writing on them, and provide no explanation as to why, they might comply in the short term. But they're used to bending rules, especially those that don't seem to make any sense. So chances are good that in a few days you'll see them back wearing logo t-shirts. But when you take it to the next level and explain, for instance, that clients or co-workers might find certain images or words offensive, and that their t-shirt could negatively impact business, your feedback takes on new meaning. You're not a grumpy out-dated boss with control issues; you're looking out for the organization, and you're asking them to do the same.

Explaining why is one of the most effective tools leaders have at their disposal. But if you abuse it, you risk losing the effectiveness. If you really don't have a good reason why you want something done a certain way, don't give the feedback. Let some things be negotiable. That way when the time comes and you really can't offer a why, whether due to confidentiality or just the pressure of time, you'll still have the trust and cooperation of your employees.

It's always a good idea to follow up constructive feedback in writing. Unless your employees have total recall, and unfortunately, few of them do, some important detail is almost guaranteed to get lost.   It also provides a visual aid, and that's important to a generation that's used to receiving an endless stream of auditory, visual and sensory stimulation. And when you've got it in writing, there can be no disputing what was said down the line.

Synchronize Your Understanding

This final step is where the partnership aspect of the dialog kicks in. Granted, if you're forced to make a correction, you likely already know the outcome you want. Usually it's for the employee to replace the undesirable behavior with an effort that you define as high performance. But you'll never win Gen Y's buy in to change if you tell them to shut up and do as they're told.   That's a direct flash back to the type of dysfunctional parent/child relationship that usually only succeeds in encouraging more of the bad behavior.

When you ask a Gen Y employee, "Tell me how you think we can work together to build on what I've just said so we can make things even more effective next time," there's no overbearing rank being pulled. There's also no recrimination for the behavior you've called into question. It's just an invite to work together to keep getting better.

And because it's an open-ended question, with no presumed answer, it encourages discussion. If you were to simply ask, "Do you understand my feedback?" you come off sounding like an authoritative parent, an approach that is guaranteed to raise the Walls of Defensiveness.   And since a question like that isn't likely to produce more than a yes or no answer, you also lose the litmus test of the employee's understanding of the criticism.

After Joan gave Blake the full run down on why his current dress was inappropriate for the office, she followed up with a question to synchronize their understanding. "Blake, do you have any questions, or anything to add, that will help us further ameliorate the situation?" Blake knew he'd been nabbed on the dress code. Joan had presented a bunch of logical reasons why his logo shirts and flip flops didn't fit office protocol. Still, she'd been really cool about it, and now she was asking for his input. This sure wasn't like any other boss he'd had; he was used to just getting yelled at.

He felt he should say something to acknowledge the equal role Joan was giving him in the conversation. He didn't really have anything productive to add, so he merely repeated a short hand version of Joan's feedback to show that he got it: "I get it now, Joan," he said, " No more logo shirts or flip flops. And yeah, I would prefer to get formal dress reminders via text. I don't really read my email all that much."

Both Joan and Blake left the meeting with a feeling of accomplishment. Joan had kept her cool and scored some major points with her Gen Y employee. And it seemed like Blake really understood the dress code and why it existed. As for Blake, he felt a new sense of respect for Joan. She wasn't the bad guy after all; she was someone he could actually talk to, and who seemed to genuinely care about what he thought. He'd miss his old clothes, but it wouldn't be that bad to switch over to solid t-shirts. The job was worth it.

BTW: Constructive Criticism Is Different from Advice

One mistake a lot of leaders make, with both Gen Y and older generation employees, is delivering advice instead of critical feedback. This just confuses the matter, raises the Walls of Defensiveness and perpetuates the problem. You may think it's nicer to phrase feedback gently by injecting words like: should, would, ought, gotta, must, and try. The problem is that by using these words your constructive criticism becomes advice:

- I wouldn't use that print shop for this project.
- If it were me, I'd get started on this right away.
- Have you tried talking to the client?
- You should probably make a few extra just in case.

There is no language in any of the above statements that indicate that the would, should, etc., is mandatory. If it's not optional then don't imply it is.

Trying to trick employees into thinking they have a choice when they really don't doesn't make the work any more enjoyable. And if they interpret your feedback as optional, and do it their way and it turns out wrong, everyone suffers.

There are five core reasons why advice negates the effectiveness of constructive criticism and raises the Walls of Defensiveness. Let's take a look.

Why Advice Doesn't Work Reason #1: Judgment

When you give unasked for advice it sends an underlying and very judgmental message of, "You're obviously not as savvy as me because if you were; you'd have already figured out what I'm telling you." You may not consciously intend to promote this message, but it's what the person on the receiving end of your advice is likely hearing.

What's more, if you continually offer unsolicited advice, there's a good chance folks will retaliate by letting you know, in no uncertain terms, about your own faults. You may think you're being helpful, or you may truly believe you know better, but you're not going to convince anyone who's stuck listening to you. The person on the other side of your endless stream of "You should...., you better..." is probably thinking, "Who the heck is this bozo to be giving me advice? He should clean up his own mess and then come talk to me."

Why Advice Doesn't Work Reason #2: Directive

When you give advice, in essence, you're telling somebody else what to do. This implies you have all the answers about what works and what doesn't. But how could you? Chances are you don't have all the background information on the situation, nor do you understand the other person's emotions and what makes them tick. This makes you anything but an expert.

There's absolutely no constructive value in statements like, "Well, if it were me, I would...." It's not you, and saying this only puts the other party on red alert as he or she checks out of the conversation to build up the Walls of Defensiveness. You asked the employee to partner in dialog, so let them talk and provide additional facts about the situation. Or if they have nothing to voluntarily offer, ask a few questions that prompt them to fill in the blanks. But be careful. Sometimes the questions we ask are no more than a thinly disguised form of unsolicited advice.

I had a recent experience where my laptop froze while I was at a client site. The client called in his tech support department and the first thing one of the IT guys asked me was, "Did you try rebooting it?" Now, that may be the question everybody asks, but it's not a question; it's really a directive, and that means its advice.

Here's the internal reaction I had to his "advice question:"

<Sarcastically> "Holy crap, you mean you can restart a laptop? Why didn't I think of that? I mean, every day I turn it ON, but I never thought about turning it OFF. They clearly don't pay you enough because that is absolute GENIUS!"

Of course, I bit my tongue and answered his question. But what if he'd instead asked me, "What actions have you taken so far?" There's a big difference between that and," Did you try rebooting it?" One is a legitimate attempt to gather information while the other, as we said, is unsolicited advice.

Why Advice Doesn't Work Reason #3: Inflexibility

When you give advice you offer the other party only two choices: take the advice or ignore the advice. If your advice is taken that

---

• • •

When It's Okay to Be Directive

We don't mean to imply you should never be directive. When you're a superior telling a subordinate what to do it's perfectly acceptable. But even in that situation, you still need to be careful that you're giving directions not advice. Because if you give advice, you're only setting the stage for a terrible dynamic.

Here's an example of what we mean:

Scenario: Boss sees Employee writing a report and says to employee:

BOSS: "I wouldn't use those colors for that report. I'd go with something brighter."
EMPLOYEE: "Sure, okay."
Later that day, after the employee has finished the report and presented it to boss, Boss says:
BOSS: "What the heck is this? I told you to use brighter colors."
EMPLOYEE: "No, you said YOU would use something brighter. I liked the colors I was already using just fine."

• • •

means the other person must tacitly admit you're right and he or she is wrong. This automatically gives you credit for being smarter. This is a dangerous scenario, and it's one that's almost guaranteed to send the Walls of Defensiveness skyward.

When advice is ignored it invites the possibility of an," I told you so," thus prompting yet more defensiveness. Even if you outwardly don't acknowledge the failure to take your advice, the person who passed on taking it may fear you're insulted. This scenario can shut someone down from attempting any future discussion on the topic (or any other topic for that matter). And then, there's always the chance that your constant advice and inflexibility has you positioned as someone to be avoided.

Why Advice Doesn't Work Reason #4: Narcissism

Let's be honest. Sometimes we give advice to demonstrate how smart we are, or because we feel left out or need to be needed. There are even cases where criticism is used to vent anger or to purposely hurt someone. But it's always done under the thinly veiled guise of trying to be helpful.

Before you offer constructive criticism, consider your reasons. If your purpose is not to help someone improve or to elicit a change, you probably want to rethink giving the criticism.

Why Advice Doesn't Work Reason #5: Unsolicited

Most advice is offered unsolicited. This means the other party didn't ask to be judged, corrected, or directed. When you catch someone off guard and

---

•   •   •

BOSS: "Listen, when I tell you to do something, I just want you to do it."
EMPLOYEE: "Then next time tell me what you want."

As a superior you have the right (and obligation) to give directions and make corrections. However, when you phrase it as advice it sounds more like a recommendation than a directive. And as we've seen, that creates a misunderstanding that wastes everyone's time.

To avoid these kinds of situations, follow the rule from Don't Skimp in the Details: If what you need to tell a subordinate is NOT optional, then be honest with them. Don't play coy and pretend *they have a choice when actually they don't.*

•   •   •

---

hit them upside the head with advice; there's virtually no chance they'll be in an open emotional state to hear what you say.

Putting It All Together

To sum up the I.D.E.A.L.S. technique, here's a quick review of the techniques and a simple script for each:

I: Invite them to partner: "Would you be willing to have a conversation with me about XYZ. Does right now work, or would you rather wait until after lunch?"

D: Disarm yourself: "I'd like to review the situation to make sure I'm on the same page as you."

E: Eliminate blame: "And if we have different perspectives, we can discuss those and develop a plan for moving forward."

A: Affirm their control: "Does that sound OK to you?"

L: List Correct feedback: "The behavior I am seeing is X,Y,Z. and what I need to see is A,B,C."

S: Synchronize your understanding: "Tell me how you think we can work together to build on this and make things even more effective next time."

Imagine the following situation: You're launching a new ad campaign and you put Joe, a Gen Y employee, in charge of finalizing the itinerary for an important client meeting. Despite the fact that you've seen several drafts of the itinerary, Joe shows up to the meeting empty handed.

You're pretty angry about this because it leaves you looking unprepared and amateurish in front of the client. You pull through the meeting and then approach Joe to discuss what happened. Below are two options for starting your conversation:

Version A

"I gotta tell you Joe, I'm pretty pissed about not having the itinerary. You obviously didn't listen when I said you were in charge of getting it done. Your

irresponsibility made me look like a total ass. If you want to sabotage your career that's fine, but don't screw up my career too. If you're not going to do something, just tell me so I can do it myself, like everything else."

Version B

"Joe, would you be willing to have a conversation with me about the missing itinerary? I'd like to review the situation to make sure I'm on the same page as you. And if we have a different perspective, which is totally possible, we'll work that out and come up with a plan for the future. Does that sound OK? Great. Do you have time now or do you want to wait until after lunch?"

Which version is likely to make Joe receptive to the message you need to deliver about his performance? And which version is sending Joe the message he's under attack and that he needs to raise his guard? The situation isn't going to get remedied until Joe changes his behavior, and you need his willing participation to make that happen. Hopefully it's clear that Version B is the preferred choice.

Here's the one comeback that some leaders have to Version B: "But I'm really pissed at Joe, and he needs to know that. He let me down and I feel betrayed. Version B makes it sound like I'm letting his behavior slide and I can't allow that."

That's a very legitimate response. We've all felt those same thoughts, and we've all had that same emotional itch to be scratched. But here's the problem: We need Joe to fix his behavior and improve his performance. And the question is whether making Joe defensive is the best way to accomplish that.

Version A is virtually guaranteed to make Joe defensive. And if his defensiveness makes him aggressive, you're going to have a fight on your hands. Remember, he's an employee,; not your indentured servant or an inmate in your prison; so you can't beat him into submission. And if he becomes passive, he'll endure your emotional browbeating, but he may subtly sabotage you down the road.

NEW RULE #3:

Work Must Have Meaning and Vision

One day a man came upon a construction site where three masons were working. He asked the first mason, "What are you doing?" In response, the mason slapped down some mortar and said, "I'm laying bricks." The man then asked the second mason the same question, "What are you doing?" The mason just shrugged and said, "I'm putting up a wall." Finally, the man approached the third mason, who was whistling as he worked. Once again he asked, "What are you doing?" The mason turned to him with a big smile and said, "I'm building a cathedral."

Past generations of workers may have been content to lay bricks and put up walls, but Gen Y wants to build a cathedral. They aren't going to follow the old rule that says employees are just another cog in the wheel. Boomer parents raised their kids with the understanding that they could make a difference and impact the world. Gen Yers have been conditioned since birth to believe that unless there's purpose behind what they do, it's not worth doing.

The best leaders recognize that Gen Y wants work that has value. But it doesn't have to be about saving the manatees or solving global warming. As we saw in the story above, laying bricks and building walls constitute the same task as building a cathedral. The only thing that's different is how the employee interprets the work. Gen Y wants to know that what they do contributes to a big picture vision. And if it isn't readily apparent, you can bet they're going to ask "Why?" Why am I doing this? Why am I this cog and not another? And why is the wheel turning so slowly?

Folks that were raised before the era of free love or even the days of the disco live by the standard that you don't question your elders. So when a seasoned leader says, "I want finished documents printed in triplicate on blue paper," the anticipated reply is, "Consider it done!" This expectation of unquestioning compliance makes Gen Y's "And why do you want me to do this?" sound pretty darn confrontational.

Without the perspective of the world in which Gen Y was raised, it's easy to perceive the question "Why?" as a challenge against authority. To followers of the old rule, asking"Why?" was typically met with frustration or even punishment. If a parent said, "Bedtime is 9:00 p.m. sharp," you learned the hard way that dragging your feet didn't change the rules. And if you asked "Why?" you were probably told, "Because I said so."

But Boomer parents took a different approach. They encouraged "Why?" and turned the question into a learning opportunity. Instead of, "Because I said so," Gen Y's explanation of bed time probably went something like this: "Kids your age need at least nine hours of sleep for muscles, skin and bones to properly grow. You've got Kindermusik at 8:00 a.m. tomorrow, and we have to drop daddy off at the train station at 7:00. So if you don't go to bed by 9:00, you're not going to get the required sleep."

Gen Y is used to asking "Why?" and getting a complete answer. They don't consider "Why?" a dirty word and they're not using it for personal attack or to snub their nose at the old rule. In fact, they have no concept of the old rule. So the next time you feel attacked by a Gen Y'ers' "Why?" call to mind the level of reasoning they're used to having behind every direction. A blunt command for triplicate copies in blue isn't going to resonate or motivate. It's just a meaningless task, and that's not something Gen Y wants to do. But take the extra 20 seconds to give them a good reason why you need triplicate copies in blue, and they'll be happy to meet your expectations.

Sense of Purpose

During the democratic primary season of 2008, Barack Obama sent a message that energized Gen Y voters. Regardless of whether you hate him or love him, there's no denying that Obama's message of, "We are the ones we've been waiting for. We are the change that we seek," directly communicated the sense of purpose the younger generation seeks.

It wasn't just another politician promising, "I'm going to make a change; I'm the one who can fix what's wrong." Obama took away the 'I' and replaced it with a 'We.' And by doing so he provided supporters with the belief that with their vote they were investing in something greater than just a candidate or a cause. He might be the leader, but they were the ones who would make a difference.

It would be great if every work task held obvious merit that proclaimed, "Do this and change the department/organization/field or even the world." But in most organizations, that's not a reality. There are always tasks that employees view as mundane, repetitive or meaningless, but which are critical to company success. But while the significance of this work may be crystal clear to a leader, it's not always quite as clear cut for employees. Smart leaders get proactive and make every job important by providing a message of purpose.

There are two main factors by which Gen Y defines work that has value:

- Meaningful Direction
- Compelling Purpose

When Darren, a top sales manager at an auto insurance agency, gives his Gen Y sales reps a task, he makes sure to let them know how their efforts will benefit the company as a whole. He recently asked two of his Gen Y employees to read through a stack of 200 completed customer surveys. A boring task that he knew would elicit Gen Y's favorite question, "Why?"

Darren preempted the interrogation by beating his employees to the punch. When he assigned the task he gave the following cogent directions that included a sense of purpose: *"We've heard that some of our customers are unhappy with our sales process. I need you guys to carefully comb through these surveys and load the results into a dashboard. Then we'll sit down as a team and use the information you culled to figure out what changes we need to make."* Because Darren provided a sense of purpose to what might be interpreted as nothing more than grunt work, his employees understood the importance of the task. They were excited about being an integral part of the change and got right to work.

Coming up with a sense of purpose can sometimes be challenging. Leaders are forced to question the reasoning and significance behind what they want employees to do and how they want it done. It becomes especially tricky when there are organizational procedures in place that have no real value. One place this sometimes shows up is in the policy governing dress code. As long as the rule makes sense, it's easy for leaders to explain why. But when there's no clear justification for the rule, things can get a bit sticky.

Ricki is the director of a tutoring company that has a strict dress policy. She doesn't just lay down the law on the white collared shirt, khaki pants and closed-toe shoes employees are required to wear, she backs it up with a sense of purpose by saying, *"No matter what school we're in, the uniform way in which we dress brands us as part of the organization. Looking professional also separates us from the kids we teach and sends a clear message that we're here in a professional capacity."* Her tutors are young, but they get the message. They understand that they need to look like grown-ups to get the respect of parents, teachers and students.

On the other hand, there's David. He manages a research firm and recently faced a very different situation. Most of his Gen Y staff, and even some of his older generation employees, began challenging the organization's no shorts, no sandals and no jeans rule. David felt they had a valid reason to question the policy since they were in a separate building from the rest of the company and clients never came to their office.

David admitted he had no idea why the policy was in place. He'd never really thought about it; he just accepted and enforced it as part of the status quo. He welcomed his employees to try and get the dress code changed. He suggested they use non- work time to research it, draft a new policy, and put together a petition and signatures. He promised he would then go to corporate with a representative and do whatever he could to help execute a change.

Addressing Gen Y's sense of purpose forces managers to look beyond what they have always accepted without contest. Of course, there are going to be tasks that just can't be changed, even if the sense of purpose behind them seems negotiable or can't be openly shared. But if you're being fair and upfront with your Gen Yers, they'll accept those times that you really do have to say, "Because I said so."

There's also a real possibility that Gen Y's challenges to the status quo will result in new decisions and better strategies that bring benefit to the organization. After all, where would Microsoft be without Bill Gates asking "Why?" And the same goes for companies like Nike, Apple and Starbucks. All these companies reached phenomenal success by turning the "Why?" to their advantage.

Providing a Vision

A lot of organizations place a vision or mission statement in front of employees and say, "This is what we do and why." But research shows this has little to no effect on employee performance or motivation. Leadership IQ did a survey of 80,000 employees to learn just how many of them could clearly articulate the goals and vision of their organization. Only 34 percent said they could. And when we followed up by asking that 34 percent to relay the company message, half of them got it wrong.

In one case, a CEO, desperate to prove us wrong, pulled a thousand dollars from his pocket and offered it to the first employee who could recite the company vision from memory. Despite the fact that the vision was stated right on the company name badge that every employee was required to wear, and that some of them had been wearing that badge for decades, not one person could meet the challenge. Obviously, that company's vision statement wasn't doing its job, and they're not an isolated case.

One major problem with vision statements, and especially as they apply to Gen Y, is that they look so far into the future that they seem static and with no real sense of purpose. The younger generation grew up in a world that embraced immediacy, so their view of change on the horizon typically doesn't extend beyond a few years. They don't want a vision that can stand the test of time; they want to be part of change that happens today. Putting a 20-year vision in front of a 20 year-old employee is like giving a 50 year-old employee a 50-year plan. It's a target that looks into the future for as long as they have been alive, and it's neither realistic nor compelling.

Gen Y wants a short-term vision that shows transformation. And that means looking no more than two to three years into the future. It has to describe not just the enduring purpose of the organization, but also what is going to change and how employee participation will impact that change.

We worked with one hospital that was having a terrible time attracting and retaining Gen Y employees. When we looked at their vision statement, here's what we found:

- To be the hospital of choice for patients, physicians and employees because of our preeminent patient care.

There's nothing in this statement that indicates an employer that offers compelling, meaningful and unique work. While it's a very nice and laudable goal, it could be talking about any hospital in the world. And that's simply not going to grab the best of Gen Y and say, "Come work for us. Here's the direction we're headed. It's really special and exciting, and you can be a valuable part of it."

When we suggested the hospital rework their vision so it would speak to the younger generation, here's what they came up with:

- Improve patient satisfaction by 30% by encouraging employees to adapt proven service best practices to our hospital and develop new practices that other hospitals will want to adapt.

This vision wasn't nearly as nicely written (the sentence structure is a bit complicated), but it did clearly tell any prospective Gen Yer where they're headed and how they could actually make a contribution in the very near future.

If you have a company vision, take a look at it from Gen Y's point of view. Does it look so far into the future that it seems unrealistic? And does it provide a clear picture of how each employee will play a role in being a part of company change? If not, it's time for a rewrite.

The key to an effective company vision is honesty. Misrepresenting your company standards or values just to make the job and the organization seem more important or interesting isn't going to work. Remember, Gen Y has been sold to all their lives and their BS monitors are state of the art. You might catch Gen Y's attention with false claims, but their information filters will quickly reveal the truth. If you can't produce what you promise, don't promise it.

How Much Is Too Much?

One question leaders often ask is how much Gen Y actually needs to know. It's one thing to give some background information to justify a task, but quite another to give full disclosure. While the answer to this question is case-by-case dependent, it's important to remember that Gen Y lives in a transparent world, and that means, one way or another, they're used to getting the whole truth.

Most of them have a Facebook or MySpace account where they're only too happy to share pictures, intimate details of their lives, and a wide range of opinions on just about anything. They're bored by static, non interactive websites and are drawn to the information sharing aspects of Web 2.0. They want an inside view and to interact, connect and participate wherever and whenever they can. Transparency is second nature to Gen Y, and they're quick to distrust those who try to cloud the truth.

Understandably, this creates a conflict for leaders who take a more rigid view on disclosure. There will always be some factors that legitimately remain on a strictly need to know basis. But opening up the files on the stuff that isn't confidential is one of the best ways to sate Gen Y's need to know "Why?" and to gain their trust. Make no mistake, most of them have the drive and the keyboard power to get the information they're after. They'll Google every executive in the organization to piece together the answers. And that can lead to some pretty dangerous conclusions.

Don't hide what doesn't need to be hidden. Instead, use it to your advantage to win the support of your Gen Y employees. They may not always agree with your decisions. But when they understand where the decision is coming from, and what inspired you to make it, they're much more likely to comply with your directions.

When Jim, the manager of a chain home appliance store, got word from the top that a recent customer survey positioned his store in the bottom percentile of acceptable customer service, he didn't shrug off the message. He was told to fix the problem, and that there would be regular, unannounced employee-performance checks. If things didn't improve, it would be his head on the plate.

Jim called an emergency staff meeting and delivered the following message, *"I'm not happy with the level of customer service around here. I see customers wandering the aisles with unanswered questions. I want every customer that enters this store to be greeted with a smile and asked if they can be helped. If you're not at a register, that means you're on the floor being actively helpful. And as customers check out, you're to ask them if they found everything they needed. I've prepared a written script of exactly how I want it said. Everyone is to learn and use this format or else face termination."*

After the meeting broke up, employees grouped off to talk about Jim's sudden crack down. *"I hear he's having problems at home,"* one worker said. *"Screw it; I'm not gonna suffer just because he's miserable in his marriage."*

"Yeah, I heard that too," another employee responded. *"Plus I hear there's an opening in corporate, and I just bet he's trying to make an impression to get the promotion. Why should we help him get ahead, especially when he just treated us like crap in that meeting?"*

Had Jim been more honest as to why he was cracking down, he could have both nipped the rumors that had no basis in truth and provided real employee motivation.

It only takes three elements to provide the level of transparency Gen Y is after. Once again, employees don't have to agree with your decisions, but if they have confidence that you used a reliable process to get there, they're almost always guaranteed to follow you.

- **Data:** What information did you use to make the decision? Maybe you spoke to customers or sent out a customer survey.
- **Input**: From whom did you get input/sources? Could be customers, corporate or even outside research.

- **Process**: What was the process you used to make the decision? This can be as simple as, "I weighed my options and took into account the pros and cons of the situation? Gen Y doesn't need a complicated answer; they just want to know how you weighed your data and arrived at your decision.

With these three elements exposed, it's easy for employees to follow the logic of a leader's decisions. And that alone can gain all the support you need.

Fulfillment

The new rule doesn't mean that Gen Y is excused from grunt work or pardoned from paying the dues of entry level work. These tasks still need to get done. But if you ask your younger workers to spend all their time laying bricks and putting up walls, they're going to lose sight of the cathedral. And that's going to result in minimal motivation.

The best leaders ensure that employees have at least some work that ignites and engages them: mind, body and soul. Work that keeps them fulfilled and meets their sense of purpose. Leaders that adhere to this strategy find it not only raises morale, but it also improves performance on the work already being done.

Google may have given it a name, but there are lots of companies that embrace a policy similar to their 20 percent time. Whether employees use this delegated time to solve existing problems or come up with new and important ideas, it allows them a project they can call their own for which they feel passion. In addition, it alleviates some of the burden on the manager to make work interesting and fulfilling; employees do that for themselves. And the bottom up innovation has proved beneficial in more cases than not.

Putting it all Together

Chuck is a 50 year-old sales manager for a nationally recognized construction equipment manufacturer. He's been with the company for over twenty years and he's seen a lot of innovation geared towards meeting the changing market. But through it all, the company has continued to pride itself on what it considers an old fashioned work ethic. The company vision, which remains as it was written in 1945, expresses this core value with the statement, "We work harder to make doing business easier."

When Chuck brought on three Gen Y new hires he expected some generational conflicts, but he wasn't prepared for all the questions, especially about work assignments. Chuck admitted there was a lot of what could be considered grunt work for new employees. Some days as many as 1,000 purchase orders came in and his new hires were in charge of printing out the orders and faxing them manually to the vendors. Chuck reasoned that it was business, and since the system had always worked just fine, who was he to question the status quo.

Evidently his Gen Yers didn't share the same sentiment. After just a week on the job they came to Chuck and asked why this job was still being done manually. Chris, the most outspoken of the new hires, spoke for the group, *"This job seems like a big waste of our time. First we have to print the purchase orders, then walk to the other side of the office where the printer is, pick up the fax, and then walk clear to the other end of the office to get to the fax machine. And there's all this paper that has to be filed, and have you seen the files? They're a total mess. It's no wonder everyone complains they can't find anything around here."*

Chuck breathed deeply. He wanted to lash out and tell these kids how easy they had it. When he started out there were no fax machines or computers. Orders were handwritten and had to be called in. They should only know what it was like to sit on hold for hours waiting to place an order with a stressed out operator and then get screamed at by the boss when the wrong order was delivered. At least now there was a paper trail to prove you made the right order.

But Chuck held his tongue. He was trying to implement the new rules, so he knew if he gave his Gen Yers a good explanation of why the job was done the way it was, and how it helped the company arrive at a big picture, he could win their support. Only when he stopped to think about it, he couldn't come up with a good reason why the system was still being handled manually. So he asked his Gen Yers what they thought could be done to improve the system.

Chris jumped right in, *"Well you know, the company vision says we work harder to make doing business easier, but what about working smarter to get the job done better and faster?"* Chuck was intrigued, so he asked Chris to go on.

"Well, there are a lot of computer based document delivery solutions out there. One of us could do the job of three if we had that without ever having to leave the desk or touch a piece of paper. I was reading on this blog the other day that the average employee uses 1.5 pounds of paper a day. With printing and everything it comes to like 6 cents a page. So we are totally working way harder than we have to, killing trees, blowing through energy, and wasting money."

Chuck had to admit that Chris not only had a valid point but a very reasonable solution. He asked his three Gen Yers if they would be interested in taking part of their work time, maybe 15 or 20 percent, to put together a proposal for what it would entail to change over to a more automated system. *"Let's shoot for going 20 % paperless to start, 40 % within a year, and a two year goal to go 100 %,"* he said. *"You guys put together the numbers and then together we'll take it to the top."*

Chuck took a giant step forward in managing his Gen Yers that day. And the company, which accepted the proposal for the way paper documents were handled, enjoyed great benefits. There were fewer errors on the documents, shipments were far more accurate, and the process took a lot less manpower. That's not to say the Gen Yers always got their way. They still continued to challenge Chuck's directions. But as long as he could provide a sense of purpose and make the tasks meaningful and unique, he never had any trouble gaining their support. And if he couldn't, he opened himself up to change.

NEW RULE #4:

Ask: "What Can *I* do for You?" Not: "What Can *You* do for Me?"

*R*umor has it that Gen Y lacks loyalty. It's not uncommon to hear seasoned leaders gripe that the younger generation feels no guilt when it comes to quitting an organization. The irony is that while the older generation is busy asking, "Why should I train someone who is just going to leave?" Gen Y is just as engaged in the question of, "Why should I stay in a job that holds no value for me?"

With the old rule there was little question about loyalty. If you took care of the organization, the organization took care of you. And even in cases where it didn't, most folks stayed put and kept giving anyway. Starting over brought significant professional risk and job changes were a resume taboo. In light of this, it's not surprising that so many leaders interpret Gen Y's loyalty to their career, rather than the organization, as mutinous behavior. But the world that sustained the old rule doesn't exist anymore, and Gen Y was right there watching as it fell apart.

The younger generation witnessed their parents give years of hard work to an employer only to see them get fired due to corporate downsizing and offshoring of jobs. Wall Street's influence on operational policy turned guaranteed retirement benefits into anything but and hazed the future of social security. A lot of factors came in to play that shattered the bond between organization and worker. And while a war for loyalty does exist, Gen Y didn't fire the first shot. They may not be willing to sign a lifetime contract with an organization, but can you really blame them after everything they've seen?

This doesn't mean leaders can't build a solid relationship with Gen Y. The old rule may be dead, but loyalty isn't. It just looks different than it used to. The best of Gen Y may not stick around forever, but given the choice of a star that stays for three years or a slacker that signs on for life, which would you prefer? The key to retaining Gen Y is giving them something to be loyal to. And we're not just talking about a pay check. Gen Yers want learning opportunities and new skills that will help advance their careers. And if you do it right, you just might hold on to them for a long time to come.

Start with Employment Ads

The new rule doesn't go into effect on the first day of work; it has to start with the job ad. Because the only way you can retain Gen Y is if you attract them in the first place. Smart leaders know that a list of all the things they can do for you isn't what Gen Y is looking for. The thing they want to know is what you can do for them.

When Cindy, the CEO of a video game company, was unable to draw in qualified candidates to fill an opening for a programmer, she went back to her job ad to look for the problem. She wanted a young, bright and technically skilled employee that she could shape and grow along with the company. But so far all she'd drawn in were under qualified candidates. And that was disconcerting given the entire ad focused on skill:

Are you a C++ Programmer who's shipped Video Game titles? Apply today to join our award winning studio.

Requirements:
Excellent C/C++
Working Experience in Game Development (at least 3 years)
Knowledge of Pixel Shaders and Vertex
Fundamental FX Skills and Techniques

Game Asset Pipelines
Strong Team and Communication Skills
Bachelors Degree in Computer Science or related

Job Description:
Development and Maintenance of current graphics engine
Working On Next Generation Platforms
Developing Visual Effects
Graphics Optimization

Benefits:
Competitive salaries - DOE
Full Benefits

Cindy reworked her ad to embrace the new rule. She didn't lose the responsibilities and requirements sections, but did change the emphasis of the ad so it focused first on what the company could do for the employee.

Here's what she came up with:

Have you been dreaming about creating the next world of Warcraft, or Call of Duty or Rainbow Six? Are you a C++ programmer or good with real time systems and love video games? Stop dreaming, start doing...read on...

What's in it for you?
Working on games!!!
Enjoying your job and your coworkers everyday
Competitive salaries DOE
Health, dental, 401k & employer matching
10 vacation days, 4 sick days, 3 personal days

What you will be doing!
Development and Maintenance of current graphics engine
Working On Next Generation Platforms
Developing Visual Effects
Graphics Optimization

What you need!

Excellent C/C++

Working Experience in Game Development (at least 3 years)

Knowledge of Pixel Shaders and Vertex

Fundamental FX Skills and Techniques

Game Asset Pipelines

Strong Team and Communication Skills

Bachelors Degree in Computer Science or related

The new rule content worked. Cindy drew in several qualified candidates and ended up with the programmer she wanted.

We sometimes get folks at our seminars that say, "Wait a minute. It's easy to lure in Gen Yers with a job like that. It's high tech and right up their alley, but what about me? My organization sorts and hauls garbage, how am I supposed to attract the younger generation to that?"

Typically, we answer the question by first taking a look at the job ad currently being used. For example:

Responsibilities: Packaging, profiling, storing and arranging for transportation of collected waste. Duties include inspections of supplies and materials received from vendors, periodic audits and report writing.

Required Skills and Experience: 2+ yrs of work experience in OSHA hazardous materials handling. Must possess excellent oral and written communication skills, analytical and creative problem solving.

Competitive Pay & Excellent Benefits!

It's unlikely a Gen Yer is going to jump at this opportunity, at least not as it's currently described. The entire focus is on what they can do for you. We talked to the manager for a few minutes to uncover the core values of the company, its vision and what it's really like to work there. It turned out to be a really cool organization that was dedicated to developing innovative ideas to stop, and even reverse, damaging environmental waste management practices.

Using this information we reworked the ad so it started with some verbiage that described a job environment and benefits that would speak to Gen Y job seekers:

Are you:

> *Committed to protecting the environment*
> *Independent*
> *Optimistic about the future*
> *Adaptable to change*
> *Peer-oriented*
> *Fast to grasp new concepts and multi-task*
> *Technologically savvy*

If so, being part of the Acme team might be the right job for you. Visit our website at Acme.com and find out how a career with Acme will give you a marketable edge in innovative solutions to heal the planet, communications, politics and environmental law.

The revised ad promises an enticing work environment and skill enhancement, but it also appeals to Gen Y's social consciousness. This is a generation that's globally aware and civic-minded. So offering them a job that allows them to do something environmentally important, gain new skills, and get paid for it; that's something that will catch their attention.

Resume Enhancement

Gen Y wants to work for an organization that leverages their talents and increases their professional market value. They live by the motto of quid pro quo: they're giving something and they want something in return. The best leaders don't wait for Gen Y to ask, *"What am I going to gain by working here?"* They take the initiative to stimulate performance and win loyalty by pointing out to employees--- on a regular basis--- exactly what's in it for them.

Some leaders are hesitant to grow their people too quickly. It seems like a huge outpouring of time, money and energy with no guarantee that the employee will stick around. But leaders that do nothing to induce Gen Y to stay more often than not see the door close behind them. The best retention rates are achieved by leaders that help employees recognize the organization as a place where they can continually polish their skills.

For Gen Y, learning is a constant process. They don't buy in to the old way of thinking that said, "I learned what I need to know and now it's time to do it." But before you start scrambling to find ways to give Gen Y the learning opportunities they want, take stock of what you're already giving them. Chances are you don't have to pay for classes or seminars to satisfy Gen Y's thirst for professional development. There's a good chance that everything they need to increase knowledge, improve core competencies, and broaden their abilities is already at their direct disposal right within the organization. They just haven't recognized it yet.

Employees learn all the time, but they typically don't realize it's happening. At least not until it's pointed out to them. Or else they move to another organization where there are no learning opportunities, and suddenly they become aware of how good they had it with you. Don't wait for Gen Y to figure it out for themselves. Take some time each month to perform a face-to-face learning review that reinforces all the opportunities their current job provides.

This doesn't have to be a time consuming process, and there's no prep period involved like there is before a yearly review. It's maybe a ten minute investment of time where you sit employees down and ask them to answer the following four questions:

- **High point:** What was your professional high point this month?
- **Low point:** What was your professional low point this month?
- **Realized:** What's something that you're better at now than you were last month?
- **Goals:** What things would you like to get better at this month?

The trick, of course, is that the employee will tell you themselves exactly what they have learned. And it's likely something that they wouldn't have gotten credit for unless you asked them to think about it. This will flick some internal switches that shine a spotlight on the value of the job.

You're also going to find out just how motivated individual employees are by how they answer the questions. A high performer will be learning things while low performers won't. What's more, the knowledge you acquire about your employees' goals and motivations, as well as what sucks the life out of them, can be used to create additional opportunities. These are all factors that will keep employees excited about the job and focused on a future within the organization.

Career Mapping

You can't expect the younger generation to sit patiently by while their professional path ambles towards an uncharted future. Gen Y doesn't believe in paying their dues in order to earn their way to the top. That's a belief system that belonged to the old rule. They come from a world of immediacy, and they want to know today exactly how they're going to reach tomorrow. But if you leave it up to Gen Y to manage their own careers, there's a good chance they'll navigate themselves right out of your organization.

At Leadership IQ, we encourage leaders to engage Gen Y employees in career mapping. Some leaders are uncomfortable helping employees plan for the future for fear it may lead them somewhere else. The fact is, employees are going to plan regardless. But without your guidance, they may not see all the opportunities that abound within the organization, and that's guaranteed to induce them to look elsewhere. Take a little time to help them figure out where they want to go and how your organization can help them get there. It gives you more control over the outcome and spotlights you as a leader who cares about employee advancement and success.

Of course, career mapping isn't all about Gen Y and giving them what they want. "Here is what you want" is a prelude to "Here is what I expect in return." The goal is to use their expectations as an opportunity to introduce a reciprocal adult conversation. If an employee tells you he or she wants a promotion and a raise, it doesn't matter if you think they deserve it or not.

It's leverage that allows you to respond with a statement like, "Sure. Let's discuss the criteria required to earn that promotion and how we can get your performance to meet those standards."

You're not saying yes, and you're not saying no. In theory, you're laying down your own quid pro quo by asking, "What are you going to do for me to earn what you want?" But at the same time, you provide the employee with an opportunity to take stock of what they want and how to get there. So they're not just hearing a parent say, "No," or a boss say, "What the heck are you thinking! You have to do something to earn that promotion!" Career mapping is a subtle way to effect a change that transforms Gen Y's quid pro quo mentality into one of, "I see. If I reach these standards then I get the reward I want."

We've developed a set of four questions for leaders to use in helping employees map their future. You may not agree with some of the answers your Gen Yers provide. They may not be feasible within the boundaries of your organization, or you may not think the employee possesses the capabilities to achieve the dream. If that's the case, delve deeper into what the employee wants and why. Uncover the motivation behind the aspiration and see if you can find alternative solutions within the company that still meet the employee's core needs.

1.   The job title, responsibilities and salary I desire:

One year from now:

Two to three years from now:

Five years from now:

2.   I want to do the job to which I aspire because (list three reasons)

1.

2.

3.

3.   I currently lack the following skills to do the job to which I aspire.

Strategies I will use to gain those skills are:

1.

2.

3.

4.

5.

4.   If this position doesn't materialize, my back up plan is:

Mentoring

Gen Y wants to work smarter, not harder. So they view learning by trial and error as fundamentally stupid. Their take is, "Why waste time making mistakes when I can just ask someone who already knows how to do this?" This throws a whole new light on what's expected from mentoring. And it's a particularly difficult concept for managers who graduated from the school of hard knocks, and who expect others to do the same.

Gen Y is great at asking for help, so encourage them to do so. That doesn't mean you have to give them all the answers. Set them up to better approach the problem, and then check in to make sure they stay on track. And remember, mentoring isn't just about giving practical advice. Satisfy Gen Y's need for positive reinforcement by letting them know when they hit on desirable performance levels.

Putting It All Together

Jane is the director of marketing for a national pizza franchise company. When she rewrote her job ad to appeal to a Gen Y audience, she found herself with several viable candidates, all of whom were excited about the promise of what the organization could do for them. She hired Josh, who was fresh out of college, to fill the role of assistant marketing coordinator.

Once Josh's basic training was completed, and he was settled in to the day-to-day aspects of the job, Jane called him into her office to talk about resume enhancement. She'd made promises in the job advertisement and during the interview process and she knew if she wanted to retain Josh, she had to keep him aware of the ways in which he was perpetually polishing his skills.

She asked him the four resume enhancement questions:

- What was your professional high point this month? To which Josh replied, *"Well, it was pretty cool when you let me help the franchisee in Tulsa through his issues. I know that we had just gone through the same problem with the franchisee in San Antonio, but it was really empowering to do it on my own. I had the information and the communication skills I needed to make a difference."*

- What was your professional low point this month? Josh answered, *"I'm sure you remember how I totally screwed up getting the campaign materials out to the new franchisee in New York. If you hadn't stepped in and saved the day, that could have gone really wrong. But I learned a lot from the experience on how to function in an emergency. I hope I never have to, but if I do, I'll be prepared."*

- What's something that you're better at now than you were last month? To which Josh responded, *"I'm getting a lot better at coordinating the different marketing campaigns. I always prided myself on being a really great multi tasker, but I realize now that it takes more than I thought."*

- What things would you like to get better at this month? Josh replied, *"I really like working one-on-one with the franchisees. I want to get better at that."*

Since Jane had Josh in her office, and the conversation was flowing nicely, she decided to launch in to their first career mapping session. She said, "I'm pleased at your progress here, Josh. You're learning fast, and as you've just told me yourself, you're already increasing your skills and your value to the organization. But I'm also interested in what you want for your future and how I can help you get there." Then she gave Josh the four career mapping questions and asked him to meet again in a day or two, after he had time to carefully answer the questions.

When they reconvened, Jane reviewed his answers and learned that Josh had a sincere interest in marketing. He saw himself in a position such as senior marketing communications manager by the end of his first or second year with the company. One day, he admitted, he'd like Jane's job, but figured it would probably take four or five years to get there.

He listed the following three reasons for his aspirations:

1. I want more interaction with people.
2. I want to develop my writing skills.
3. I want more visibility within the organization.

There was nothing listed under 'skills lacking.' Josh had only written, "Not sure."

As for his back up plan, Josh wrote, "I think I could do well in sales. I've been watching the work they do and it's intriguing. I might also like to utilize my journalism studies from college and find a job with a newspaper."

Jane got right to work. *"Communications Manager is a good goal to have,"* she said. *"That position means you are one of the main liaisons between the franchisees and corporate. There's a lot of stuff you have to know, like contracts and budgets. Why don't you put together a list of skills you'll need in order to get that job and figure out ways for you to gain that experience in your current position. That will fill in the blanks where you didn't know the skills you lacked."*

Josh was excited that Jane didn't pan his dreams as he'd expected. He had a few buddies that worked for other companies, and they were having a really hard time getting through to their bosses about where they wanted to be even a year from now. He could hardly wait to tell them he had a boss that was willing to help him not just get ahead, but to one day possibly even take her job.

As they were wrapping up, Jane called Josh's attention to the fourth question. *"If you really have interest in sales, we might be able come up with a few fun things you could do to assist over there. They always need the help, and I think you'll enjoy working with them. That way you get a little experience under your belt should you one day chose to go that route. I also think we can come up with some creative strategies to work in more of your writing skills. We can work it into your 20 percent time if you like."*

Josh walked out of the meeting feeling good about his future with the organization. He hadn't been sure about the job, writing was his first love. But if Jane could work that in and give him all the other stuff she had promised, he had no problem sticking around.

NEW RULE #5:

The Work World is a Social Community

e work with one digital media technology company which uses the tag line, "A job should be more than just a job," as an integral part of their recruitment pitch. If you go to the careers page of Atlas Solutions' website, you won't find an overload of "requires this, requires that, don't bother applying unless." What you will find is fun information about the people who work for Atlas and the company culture they enjoy.

Job seeking visitors are first attracted to the flash game, "Beat the Man Down." Players select from an array of office weapons (everything from giant staplers to water cooler jugs) and get a chance to go one-on-one with the quintessential "bad boss." After blowing off a little steam, visitors move on to the comical, Top 10 Reasons You Should Look for a New Job. Then there are employee candids that include shots of folks doing all sorts of goofy fun stuff like mechanical bull riding accompanied with captions like: "Work hard, play hard." And then there's the flashing banner that introduces some statistical factors regarding the company culture, such as:

- Szechwan Noodle Bowl Fan Club: 15 and growing
- Ultimate Frisbee Players: 10
- Ranking of favorite out-of-work activities with coworkers:

- o Karaoke
- o First Wednesday society
- o Trivia contests
- o Motorcycle riding
- o Champ Karts
- # of Atlas employees who have run marathons and competed in triathlons: 6
- # of Atlas employees who have imagined running marathons: 200

It's obvious that, at Atlas, work is also a social outlet. And because they're one of our clients, we can factually state that in spite of the fact that employees have fun on the job, the company remains successful. The company culture at Atlas couldn't be further from the old rule that said: "You're being paid to work, not socialize. If you want a friend, go buy a dog." By the way, it should be noted that Atlas is a subsidiary of Microsoft (also a client). So whether you're an intimate environment or a Fortune 500 behemoth, you too can create a job that's more than just a job.

Back in the day, which wasn't all that long ago, employees who had fun or were caught socializing on the job were frowned upon. They may as well have been stealing from the company. Sure, there were a few bones tossed in like the annual Christmas party or a company barbeque each summer, but nothing that raised morale on a day-to-day basis. Older generation workers may not have liked the environment, but since questioning the status quo wasn't an option, they managed the emotional drop off from "life" to "work" as best they could.

Not surprisingly, Gen Y doesn't respond the same way. From Facebook to blogs to Twitter, their lives are filled with constant social networking. They see no logic to checking their sense of fun and friendship at the door as they enter the workplace. And if a job just says "No," and provides no padding to ease the emotional drop off from the social life they're used to, Gen Y isn't going to produce.

Anger Is A Little Hypocritical

We need to make one additional comment about this. We hear gripes on a fairly regular basis about Gen Y's need for work to be "fun" and "enjoyable" and "fulfilling," as though those were horrible concepts. "It's called work for a reason," people often snark with bitterness dripping from their lips.

But here's our retort. Where is it written that work has to suck? Why can't work be enjoyable? Not long ago, the elderly had three basic options for living situations in the last few years of their life. If they were lucky enough to have a deeply caring family, they could live with (or near) them. If they didn't have that option, they could move into a dark, dank nursing home and wither away in an institution that looked like it had formerly housed the criminally insane. Or, they could just live alone and let solitude and despair filch their will to live.

Of course, there are other options, but far too many elderly found themselves in one of those last two options. So what did today's Boomers do? They created a whole new class of retirement communities and assisted living facilities. They refused to accept that the last years of life had to be painful and lonely. Instead, they said, "Let's build ourselves a four-star hotel complete with onsite nurses and doctors. Then we'll load it with every fun activity known to man and invite all our friends so we'll never be alone."

Now, call us crazy, but it sounds like Boomers have done to retirement what Gen Y is trying to do to the workplace. And it's pretty ironic that Boomers do more griping about Gen Y's need for "fun and friends" than any other generation. We're not saying you have to sell all your conference tables and replace them with foosball tables. But before we get too critical of Gen Y's desire to make work a fun place to be, let's at least explore whether it's possible to do great work while extracting an extra ounce of fulfillment. And remember, in general, the companies that are regarded as enjoyable places to work often generate a lot more profit than places that are not.

Ease the Drop-Off

Try to imagine what it's like for your new employees on their first day of work. They're nervous, discombobulated, and unsure of where to go and what to do. They are desperately hoping that someone will reach out and welcome them in. Given your anxiety and how much time and money you spend on new hires, it would seem like a good idea to make their first few days as warm and welcoming as possible.

But in most organizations that doesn't happen. Typically, there's nobody waiting at reception to greet a new employee upon arrival. After an awkward wait, he or she gets taken to an office that's likely missing some pretty important items (like a computer). Left alone to wait, the new hire sits there until the boss rushes by and hurriedly says, "Great to see you. I'm tied up in some meetings right now, but HR will swing by with all the paperwork stuff and then let's catch up later."

Fellow employees may walk by, but they're likely completely unaware that someone new is starting today. When the new hire finally receives some human interaction, the one message heard above all others is: "You may have been hot stuff where you came from, but here, you're at the bottom of the food chain. So shut up, listen, and maybe after a long while you'll earn the right to speak up in a meeting."

As bad as all this is, it actually gets even worse. Because while this would be a bad start for anyone, it's especially demoralizing when contrasted against the experience most folks have when checking out of their last job. Those final days of work usually involve a lot more socializing than working. Departing employees might get a pizza party, happy hour, hugs, tears, and all the rest. People they didn't even particularly like stop by and promise to "keep in touch" and "get together sometime."

Most employees that go from the last job high to the new job low fall off the emotional cliff. But Gen Y tends to fall harder than most. The younger generation is used to being in constant contact with their friends and being told how smart and wonderful they are. They're also used to having fun. And when they have to fill out forms, they're usually online and easily completed with cut-and-paste or "autofill" tools.

The typical new job experience we described above leaves Gen Yers emotionally isolated and friendless. They're told very clearly that they're on the bottom rung. Memorizing HR policies is not fun, and whatever forms they have to complete are probably arduous and shortcuts are strictly prohibited.

Ritz-Carlton managers have come up with a system that bucks the emotional fall off, and there's a valuable lesson for all leaders in their practices. Within three days of accepting a job, or being "selected" to use the Ritz parlance, a Ritz-Carlton manager is on the phone to the new hire. This early orientation hit initiates the employee's relationship with the organization. The contact is reassuring and the tension about all the unknowns on the first day starts to melt.

A second phone call is made by the manager a week prior to employee orientation. The call reconfirms the date, time, location and dress code for orientation, but it's also a gentle reminder that the employee is now part of a team; one that prides itself on attention to detail. Enthusiasm is kept high and the new hire is exposed to the Ritz's gold standard of excellence which they will soon be expected to uphold.

Third contact takes place with another phone call a few days after orientation. By now, new hires are beginning to live the culture of the Ritz, and they haven't even started work yet. Final contact takes place a few days prior to the employee's start date. Questions are answered and date, time, location and dress are reconfirmed.

The Ritz Carlton doesn't allow for any emotional drop off. The first day an employee walks on the job, they already feel like a part of the team and the company culture.

The Real Work-Life Balance

There's a lot of buzz going around about the younger generation's unrealistic demand for a work-life balance. Google that three-word phrase and you'll find plenty of arguments against the younger generation. Word is they want perks like flexible work schedules, workdays that start at noon and the option to work from home. Factors that some leaders deem are nothing more than a flimsy cover for a lousy work ethic.

Sadly, these leaders are getting hot under the collar for nothing. The work-life balance Gen Y seeks doesn't mean fewer hours or doing half the job for full salary. They want to work, they just don't want to work chained to the old rule that says you can't be relaxed, have fun and get your work done too. Atlas knows this, as do organizations like Google, Nike and Apple. At companies like these, employees walk in to a custom community built around the workplace. They won't hear, "If you want a friend go buy a dog." And in some cases, like at Google, if they already own a dog, they're welcome to bring it to work.

The best leaders create a culture of work-life balance by finding ways to fill the chasm of the non-work life to work-life shift. They welcome and encourage social experiences that lighten up the old oppressive 'nose to the grindstone' atmosphere of the workplace. And in return for emotionally satisfying the younger generations' need for a fulfilling social environment, they get enhanced employee performance and loyalty.

The military has been filling the gap for ages. The single best thing they do is basic training. That's where they strip away everything that came before and replace it with an environment that is 100 percent focused on team. Love of country and patriotism are all well and good, but that's not what inspires a soldier to charge a hill knowing death may be waiting at the top. It's "one army-one team-one fight," and it's love for the rest of the team that makes the prospect of death worth risking.

Of course, unless you're the military, you probably don't have a life or death scenario to offer as incentive, no matter how dedicated you are to your organization. And most folks aren't looking for a work environment that equals boot camp. However, there's one valuable lesson to be learned from basic training. You can't wipe away Gen Y's love of community unless you replace it with an alternate community.

It's not uncommon for leaders to shun the idea of enhancing the work place with Gen Y friendly perks. It seems like a lot of effort just to meet one more Gen Y demand. But it's not just the younger generation that scores one for the team by acting as a catalyst for a changed workplace environment. What many organizations have already found out is that when you go the extra mile to give employees the social extras they crave, it gives leaders additional control.

Not every organization is going to be like Google, complete with a Googleplex headquarters that boasts laundry rooms, swimming pools, a sand volleyball court and eleven gourmet cafeterias. But every organization can focus some attention towards creating an environment that attracts, engages and energizes the younger generation. It doesn't take enormous financial outlay to create a social world that keeps employees closely linked to the organization. And when your employees are content in their environment, they're less likely to get sucked away by the outside world. Because the fewer things they need to do "out there," the more time they're going to spend with you.

The other benefit of creating a new social work world is that it becomes a built in high performer selection bias. If you build your company environment so it appeals to the top talent you want, those are the folks you're going to attract. And of course, at the other end of the spectrum, that same environment will also completely turn off the low performers you don't want.

For example, if you promise a company car and a gas card to go with it to every new employee, odds are that anyone looking for a job will apply. That's a perk that would appeal to almost anyone. But what if you take a look at your current high performers and uncover their common links and interest. You might find that healthy, fun, team spirited and athletic are all terms that describe your best employees.

In response, you can enhance your company culture with perks like an employee dodge ball team, rafting, hiking and ski trips, gym memberships, and an office kitchen that is stocked with healthy foods. That's not the sort of environment that's going to herd in the average beer guzzling couch potato. But it is going to attract folks that share the same healthy, fun and active interests as your current high performers.

Marilyn owns a busy restaurant in small, community-oriented town. A large majority of her staff is made up of local high school students. She's had some really good luck and some really bad luck with her hiring choices. Not surprisingly, she's found that the performance level she gets from honor students far exceeds that of students who score lower grades. In an effort to attract the high performers she wants, Marilyn came up with a few job perks to act as bait.

For every eight hour shift worked, Marilyn gives her student employees a paid hour of homework time. The hour has to be done at the restaurant, but there's a little study area set up in the back where employees can also take their staff meal. And every time a student employee brings in a report card that makes honor roll, there's an automatic raise. High school kids being the master social net workers that they are, word of the job perks got around quickly. The next time Marilyn put a help wanted sign in the window, she had every job seeking honor student in town show up to apply. What's more, she didn't get the lower performing students she didn't want to hire.

There's no cut and dry rule about what makes the right social environment for the workplace. Each employer needs to look at the unique qualities of the people they want to attract and retain and create incentives that will appeal to this specific demographic.

A Universal Perk: Collaboration

Gen Y grew up with a support system that included family, parents, teachers, coaches and friends. If they had questions or problems, someone was always there to help figure it out. And it wasn't just face-to-face time. Technology allowed the younger generation to access constructive input any time they wanted it. This early experience makes it second nature for Gen Y to work in groups where they can share and expand upon their ideas and talents. They don't want to work alone, and in most organizations, collaboration is a fairly easy perk to establish.

The first step is redefining the old rule about team work. Most organizations have a Gen X oriented view of employee collaboration where everyone comes together with the purpose of dividing up the work. Then each individual goes off to do their share of the work alone. Finally, the whole group reassembles and the pieces are put together.

That's not the kind of group effort Gen Y wants to be a part of. In fact, they see meetings like this as a total waste of time; nothing is getting done. Gen Y actually works together, from start to finish. They go into a room or log into a chat room and combine efforts in a real-time collaboration. And now, they've also got the ultimate team tool: the Wiki, an online data base that can be written and edited collaboratively.

It's probably not going to excite your older generation employees if you suddenly announce a full-time swap to a Gen Y definition of teamwork. And if you ask them to do all their work using Wiki's open-editing format, there's a good chance they'll revolt. The older generation is too accustomed to working alone. However, every so often you can throw in a Wiki project or even introduce what we call a No Homework Team and not stir up a ruckus.

A No Homework Team is where you take care of business, as a group, right there right then, with no take-away work.

Joel is the creative director for a Las Vegas tourism magazine. He manages a design department with eight employees: four of them are Boomers and Gen Xers, the other half are Gen Y. The older generation employees prefer to get their assignments and do their work solo, but his Gen Yers are eager to collaborate.

Joel sees no reason why he can't give everyone what they want. For example, when the magazine needed an advertorial to cover the best restaurants in Las Vegas, Joel called a No Homework meeting. He ordered in lunch for the group and told them to brainstorm and write the finished product---as a group--- by the end of the day.

The mix of generations inspired input and ideas that covered a wide range of culinary interests. When the client got the finished copy for final approval they were thrilled. Joel's Gen Yers loved the experience and even his Xers and Boomers had to admit that it was a productive and fun way to get the job done.

But not all projects merit a group effort. Joel keeps his older generation team members happy by also assigning work that is completed on an individual basis. By mixing it up he's able to keep everyone on his team focused and engaged.

Putting It All Together

Steve owns a PR agency headquartered in a seaside resort 100 miles from a big city. A large part of his client base consists of entertainment venues that serve a young, affluent and celebrity-oriented crowd. Steve considers himself pretty hip for a 50 year old, and he likes a good time as much as the next guy. But he's not always in the know when it comes to the younger generation's party scene. To compensate, he fills the company's support roles with Gen Yers. The bottom up innovation they bring to the table is fresh and on the mark with what his clients want.

But while Steve wants young employees that know what's hot and what's not, he doesn't want people that are living that life night after night. He has an invested interest in seeing his employees bright eyed and coherent each morning. In order to attract the right Gen Yers, Steve created a work environment that singles out the folks he wants from those he doesn't want.

He's noticed that his most responsible Gen Y employees dote on their pets, so he created a pet-friendly work space. He's found that when employees don't have the pressure (or the excuse) to run home and walk the dog, they lose their fixation on slipping out the door exactly at 5 o'clock.

At the request of his team, Wednesday is game day. Unless there is an urgent deadline, time is set aside for a game of Scrabble or Scategories, activities he's found that hold no interest for the party hounds. Birthdays are celebrated in style, and at the end of the busy summer season, the whole office enjoys a spa day followed by a picnic on the beach. Again, nothing that lends to an atmosphere that would attract the "Gen Y goes wild" bunch.

Steve encourages collaboration and starts every week with a Monday morning staff meeting. He also selects some projects to be done as a group effort. His older generation employees were a little hesitant at first to take part in the No Homework teams, but they've actually come to enjoy them. The company is slowly incorporating the use of Wiki's to centralize and organize information and reduce the number of project meetings. Not only do his Gen Yers enjoy using fun technological tools at work, but it's easy for Steve to monitor what's going on in each account by logging in to a Wiki.

It's a great work environment filled with like minded souls of all generations. Steve gives his clients the service they want, and he's happy going to work each day and enjoying the family environment he's developed.

NEW RULE #6:

Being Professional Means Getting Personal

*H*istorically, a bold line separated personal and professional in the relationship shared by employer and employee. The old rule decreed that it was career suicide for leaders to let down their guard and give subordinates an intimate view of who they were and the factors that had shaped their professional life. Aside from company conjecture and rumor, as far as employees knew, the boss was born sitting at the top. And while leaders may have found their perch a bit lonely at times, they kept mute, trusting that the mystery commanded respect.

But all that changed as technology engendered a new world of radical transparency. And while it may have started in the virtual world, it didn't take long to hit the real world, and especially the workplace. Leaders that were caught off guard in some cases paid dearly as hidden evidence of scandal or suspicious behavior suddenly became public knowledge. And those that tried to deflect the blast with silence found the old rule only made them look suspicious and even dishonest.

Leaders that were facing the firing line discovered that the only effective way to fight back was to speak out and tell their story in the most direct, immediate and transparent way possible. And so a new rule was born that said the more authentic information you share, and the sooner you reveal it, the better. Bottom line, folks aren't willing to hang around and wait for your story to unfold, not when they can access any number of searchable data bases to get the information they want. Fact or fiction, they'll take what they can find and turn it into a story of their own. You've got to beat them to the punch and deliver the facts first.

While older generation leaders scrambled to address the new rule and positively manage their on line reputations, the younger generation took it all in stride. They grew up with the technology and have spent their whole lives letting it all hang out. Most Gen Yers have a web of friends with whom they share reciprocal record of even the most mundane aspects of day-to-day life. Whether it's routine or risqué, from blog posts, to photos on Flickr, to open linking with associates, their lives are an open book.

Love it or hate it, transparency is here to stay and Gen Y isn't going to adapt to an old-rule boss. Transparency equals trust, and they want access to a behind the scenes look that shows the human side of their superiors. But while they don't expect the same emotional free-for-all from the person in charge as they do from their friends, they do want authenticity. This can provide a challenge to older generation leaders that deem public sharing as unproductive and even dangerous. But making a strategic workplace move towards transparency is a far cry from the full disclosure found on popular social networking sites.

The new rule doesn't mean you have to strip down and get emotionally naked in front of you workforce. Rather, it's a tool that allows you to leverage Gen Y's love of radical transparency to gain employee loyalty and trust. A recent Leadership IQ study on trust in the workplace showed that only 34% of employees trust their direct boss. But that number doubles for those that can say, "I understand who my boss is as a person, including his/her values and motivations." And when you stop to consider everyday language such as, "He's okay, I know him," or, "It's not that I don't trust her, I just don't know her," it makes sense that the more employees know about you, the more likely they are to trust you.

Creating an Authentic Leadership Story

Gen Y grew up with a surplus of immediate information at their fingertips. As a result, they're geniuses at distilling essential information and discarding the rest. It also means they've got a rather short fuse when it comes to attention span. If they have to wait too long for you to make your point, or there's no hyperlink to what they really want to find out, they'll filter you out with lightening speed. It's not that Gen Y finds fault with logic, but if you try and placate them by shoving a load of dry numbers, boring facts and vague concepts down their throats, you're going to lose their attention, and their trust.

Gen Y wants more than data, they want to know who you are and how you got there. Leadership stories are an easy and effective method of giving Gen Y the information they want. These palpably real and personal tales allow leaders to impart an insider view that attracts the younger generation's interest and attention. And once you've got your employees on the hook, getting them to follow you is easy. You control the outgoing stream of information, and while employees are still left to draw their own conclusions, the outcome is based on the facts you've chosen to share. But good story telling requires skill. Gen Yers don't have the same years of experience as you do from which to draw. So if your story doesn't make sense in the context of their life, they're going to tune out.

Luckily, every leader has a story that will capture Gen Y's interest. These folks are just starting out in their careers. As we've already explored, they're eager for success and they want to find the quickest route to the top. The story of your professional rise, including the values that guided your actions and the decisions you faced getting there, holds answers to their questions. A good Leadership story humanizes the boss to Gen Y employees, but it also impresses a set of desirable performance standards. Like any good story, there's a lesson to be learned: "Do what I did, the way I did it, and find success."

Since not everyone is a born storyteller, we've created four Storytelling Rules that will help you tell your tale so it keeps the interest of a Gen Y audience:

- Find the right voice
- Use experiential language
- Apply 5 Stages of a Good Story
- Eliminate the extraneous

Storytelling Rule #1: Find the Right Voice

Telling your story from the viewpoint of "I" with a first person narrative provides a sense of confessional intimacy that intrigues listeners. It allows for clear and honest revelation of the feelings, thoughts and experiences that Gen Y needs to process the personal insight they're after. It may make you feel a lot less vulnerable to tell your story from the third person, but in doing so you risk losing the effectiveness.

Look at how a change in voice affects the impact of the following story told by the CEO of an advertising company:

Third Person:

"Employees who entered this organization thirty years ago walked into a much different situation than you see today. Individual employees didn't even have their own typewriters, so it was a challenge to meet work requirements. The receptionist at the time was utterly unreliable, so entry level employees had to fill in for her. Oh, and ask any old timer about the phone system; it never worked."

First Person:

"When I first started with the company I was just a punk kid trying to make something of myself. This place was primitive; you should have seen it. There was only one typewriter that actually worked and everyone used to fight over it. I went to the library at lunch to use the typewriter there just so I could get my work done. Oh, and the phone system was totally unreliable. I'd be talking to a client and all of a sudden someone else's call would cut in, like a party line. We also had this receptionist, Lucy, who showed up when she felt like it, and for some reason nobody did a thing about it. So most days I sat at the front desk to cover for her. But you know, I was happy to do whatever to keep things running, and I learned a lot from it. Besides, from where I was coming from, it seemed like I'd hit the big time."

Which version of the story would you rather hear?

Storytelling Rule #2: Use Experiential Language

A great story draws listeners in by showing, not telling them the course of events. Telling is just the dry communication of facts and figures. But when you show through rich visualization, you encourage a sense of understanding that allows your listener to discover the experience as if it were happening to them. And just like reading a great novel, while your listeners are waiting to find out what happens next, they are also pondering what their next move would be.

Experiential language is a key function of story telling, and unlike the author of a novel, you have an advantage: the intimate knowledge of your audience. Even if it's a fairly new hire, if you've started the steps towards career mapping, you have an idea of the professional goals the employee is after. Your story might not directly reflect the one he or she wants to create, but you can still touch on core emotions that trigger a connection.

There are two reliable methods of bringing your listener into the experience:

- 5 senses: sight, touch, smell, taste and sound
- 5 core emotions: mad, sad, glad, afraid and ashamed

First, let's take a look at a story that tells instead of shows. Here, the CEO of the advertising agency is relaying to a Gen Y employee his first big break:

> *"It was a really depressing atmosphere in the office and I put in over a year without any real challenging work. But then one day my boss got called away on a family emergency. I'd been helping him pull together a big campaign for an important client and I was the only one who knew what was going on. The CEO of the company asked if I could finish the work, and while I was scared to death, I said, yes. The rest is history."*

Now let's look the same story when the events are shown instead of told. Our CEO knows the employee to whom he's telling his story aspires towards a leadership position. During their last career mapping session, he also expressed an interest in starting his own business as a back up plan.

"Still, there were some days that first year when I had to drag myself into the office. There were twenty of us squeezed in to a windowless space that was made to accommodate ten. The chair I sat in was a second hand cast off and I could feel the nails pinching into my skin. I guess I was lucky that I didn't have to sit much because I was usually making copies for someone. There was this big clock that hung over the copy machine and all day long I would feed in paper and listen to this tick tock tick tock that never ended. I'd go home and the sound would still be pounding in my ears.

Then one day my boss' wife was in a car accident. I was with him when he got the call; you've never seen anyone turn so pale. So he goes running out without telling anyone what's going on. I'm left all alone; the only one who knows anything about this big campaign we'd been working on for a top client. I had to go to his boss and explain. And there I am standing in the CEO's office with all this fancy mahogany furniture shining up at me, and he's slouched down in this red leather chair that's so overstuffed it looked like he's perched on a cloud. It's only 10 a.m. and he's puffing away at this stinky cigar and he won't even look up at me as I stand there sweating bullets and trying to sound intelligent.

Finally, he put down his cigar in this spotless crystal ashtray, and he looks up at me with these bloodshot eyes and says, "Well kid, do you think you can pull the rest of this campaign off on your own?" Man, did my head start spinning with all the things I didn't know how to do. But I took a deep breath and somehow got out the words to tell him I could do it. I walked away feeling like I was floating three feet above my body; I was petrified and elated at the same time. I knew this was my chance to prove what I was worth. It was hell, but I pulled it off, and I knew that if I could do that, I could do anything. And all of a sudden people knew who I was around here."

Storytelling Rule #3: Apply 5 Stages of a Good Story

Good stories are built on conflict and an element of suspense. Listeners gain a deeper understanding of the storyteller when they're privy to the inner struggles that were the catalyst behind important decisions. There are 5 stages to a good story:

- Scene: sets the stage for the action about to take place
- Provocation: the moment that says this is a story worth listening to
- Struggle: the mental or physical battle being waged
- Resolution: how the story ends
- Moral: the lesson learned

Let's see how our CEO applies the 5 stages:

"When I first started out it was all about the power. No matter what it took or who I had to step on to get there, I wanted to rise to the top and be a big shot. I wanted the flashy car, expensive suits and to sit in that big leather chair and smoke cigars while everyone else toiled away beneath me.

But then, I watched what happened to my boss after his wife's accident. She had trouble walking and talking, and when he couldn't be there he had to hire someone to take care of her. He went from being this total go getter that spent weekends at the office pushing himself beyond any reasonable limits to this shell of a guy who was hanging on to his job by a thread. I'm sure if it hadn't been for the situation they would have fired him. Eventually he quit. I never found out what happened to him or his wife.

Anyway, when he left it opened up a big opportunity for me. But something inside of me had changed and I was really questioning the kind of leader I someday wanted to be. Like what if something life threatening happened to me or to someone I loved; would the car or a big expense account make it all okay?

I stopped wanting to be the guy in the red leather chair. Instead, I wanted to be a leader that cared about his team and who was an integral part of the system. You know, there's nothing I would ask you to do that I wouldn't do or haven't done myself, and I hope that shows in my actions. I think about my old boss all the time, what became of him, and how he felt about all those years he spent wrapped up in his work while his wife was still healthy and happy. It's just not worth it, you know. I mean, I love my job, but I love my life as well, and I don't expect it to be any different for my team."

Storytelling Rule #4: Eliminate the Extraneous

Before you move in for the kill and tell your story, reexamine the details to make sure it accomplishes the goal you set out to achieve. Remember, your purpose is to build a bond of trust with your employee. If you've got factors in the story that are only there to address your own issues, they serve no real purpose and can even hinder the effectiveness of your story.

The Four Leadership Stories Gen Y Wants to Hear

While most leaders have a plethora of stories to share, there are four stories that will have the biggest impact on your Gen Y employees:

- **How did you get started?** This allows employees that are just beginning to forge their professional path feel a sense of kinship with you. You're no longer just the boss; you're a human being that has faced similar challenges, and even more important, you've got the know how to teach them to do the same.

- **What are your values?** Gen Y was raised to be idealistic and to believe they can make a change. The rules you chose along your own path that guided your actions in the world tell them a lot about the kind of person you are. They don't want to work for a ruthless cutthroat boss; they want to know you care and that you're personally willing to do something to contribute and make a difference.

- **How did you get to where you are?** This isn't about the years you dedicated to the organization waiting for your turn, but rather about the skills you had to develop to get to the top. Gen Y wants to learn the short cuts to success. They see no merit in learning from their own mistakes; they'd rather learn from yours.

- **Where are you headed?** Nothing is stagnant in Gen Y's fast moving world. They're looking for change to take place in a short window of time, and they want to know that you're going to deliver the goods.

Putting It All Together

Leadership stories alter the vision employees have of you as a leader in an untouchable place of authority. It's an intimate view, albeit one that you choose to share, by which your Gen Y employees can make a connection and see you as someone who is empathetic to their quest for success. When they realize that you've made some mistakes along the way, and that you're willing to admit it, you'll gain their trust. You're not telling them what to think or believe about you, but rather, your story gives them the information they need to draw their own conclusions.

You don't have to have great comedic timing or an impressive vocabulary to be a great story teller. Your life, and the journey you took to get to a position of leadership, is fascinating all on its own, especially to listeners that want to achieve the same. Just stay honest and keep it in the first person. Have some fun and use language that shows instead of tells. Make sure you follow the 5 stages of a good story, and eliminate anything that detracts from the purpose of the story.

Conclusion

*F*rank has been an employee with Company A for thirty years. He likes his suit and tie, and he's fine with the structure of the old rule workplace where he shows up, does what he's told, and everyone stays happy. He takes his yearly review seriously and makes a concerted effort to meet his boss' standards of high performance. In ten years, Frank will start thinking about retirement, but until then, the status quo is just fine with him.

Joe is fresh out of college and has only been with Company A for six months. He's a fan of t shirts, blue jeans and high-tech gadgets, and has already made several suggestions to the boss about upgrading the company technology to ease the work load. His input has been received with respect and he sees change taking place because of it. He's working on a three-year plan for advancement with his boss' assistance, and if all goes well, Joe sees a future for himself with Company A. And if the plan falls through, he's got some strong connections at Company B.

Ken is the boss at Company A. He's thrilled to report that while he takes a different approach in some aspects of how he manages Frank and Joe, they're both high performers. A year ago, he would have told you it was impossible; that Gen Yers were no more than self centered, spoiled, praise hungry vultures that fed off the workplace until a better offer caught their interest. But as his older generation workers started to retire, Ken had no choice but to learn how to accept and manage the younger generation.

Attracting, retaining and motivating Gen Y is a topic that today's leaders can no longer avoid. Those that find the best ways to harness the younger generation's talents are going to come out the winners in the war for talent. But you'll never succeed in getting their interest if you don't first address their needs. The six new rules we've outlined are a strategy any leader can use to create workplace solutions that keep Gen Y employees engaged and inspired.

Every generation has struggled to define the balance in how they live, play and work. But Gen Y's influence is creating a workplace environment that simultaneously encourages all three. The trend is happening right now, and that means there's no time to waste. We know change is scary, but it's not nearly as scary as failure. And for organizations that ignore the new rules, failure is almost guaranteed.

The Best Way to Start

Gen Y is actually on to something valuable with their question of Why? When there is a reason behind our actions it makes what we do, including instigating change, more comfortable. And that usually means we act with greater conviction. Remember, Gen Y has a super sonic "B.S." barometer, so if you throw in a few gratuitous perks just because you read them here or saw someone else doing them, it's not going to ring true.

As you work on implementing the new rules, don't lose sight of the six developmental experiences that shaped the younger generation:

- Self esteem
- Power
- Technological authority
- Immediacy
- Customization
- Concurrency

These are your reasons why; because if you want reach Gen Y, you have to remember and honor where they are coming from.

You also need to honor who you are and what you're comfortable doing. There's a lot room for creativity in each of the new rules, and we've tried to offer a wide variety of examples to show the different ways that leaders have embraced them. How you chose to implement the new rules will largely depend on what fits your personal style, what your organization is capable of providing, and what the high performance Gen Yers you seek want. But as long as you keep it authentic, and don't lose focus of the core purpose of each of the six rules, you can't go wrong.

New Rule #1: Real Time Positive Reinforcement- Look for teaching moments. Catch your Gen Yers in the act of doing something right and reward their high performance with positive reinforcement that details the skills and abilities you want to see again.

New Rule #2: Two-Way Constructive Criticism- When you need to criticize, don't kill Gen Y's all important self esteem. Make them an active part of a blame free communication that's focused on collectively finding a solution.

New Rule #3: Work Has Meaning and Vision- Don't let Gen Y employees lose sight of the cathedral they are helping to build. Be prepared to answer why? And let them know how the job has immediate meaning, vision, direction and purpose.

New Rule #4: What You Can Do for Them- Assign work that leverages Gen Y's talents and increases their professional market value. Reinforce all you have to give with learning reviews and career mapping that keeps employees focused on a future with your organization.

New Rule #5: Work Can Be Fun- Ease the emotional drop off by creating a fulfilling and collaborative environment that appeals to the high performers you want.

New Rule #6: Get Personal- Let Gen Y see that you're more than just a boss. Become someone they look up to and respect through leadership stories that appeal to their own dreams of success.

For Gen Y, the old rules are obsolete, and that means a job has to be more than just a job. Luckily, the new rules are easy to implement, and they don't require a lot of time or money.

There's one final Gen Y quality we haven't mentioned yet, and that's optimism. The younger generation doesn't have the cynicism of your older generation employees. So as long you continue to make a concerted and honest effort towards change, they'll continue to believe in you.

About the Authors

Mark Murphy, Chairman & CEO of Leadership IQ

Mark Murphy is the leading expert on training organizations how to manage Generation Y. He is the Founder & CEO of Leadership IQ, a top-rated management training company, and his training clients include Microsoft, IBM, GE, MasterCard, Merck, AstraZeneca, MD Anderson Cancer Center, and hundreds more.

Mark leads one of the largest leadership studies ever, and his groundbreaking work has appeared in Fortune, Forbes, Business Week, Investor's Business Daily, The Washington Post, The Los Angeles Times, and many more.

He's a widely recognized management authority and has appeared on ABC's 20/20, CBS News, Fox Business News and NPR.

Previously, Mark was President of a joint venture with Mercer Human Resources Consulting. And before that he was an executive at VHA, Inc., a 6-time winner of Fortune's "Best Places to Work" Award. He holds an MBA from the University of Rochester with advanced work at the Wharton School of Business.

Mark Murphy is a top-rated speaker, and has spoken at hundreds of conferences worldwide. Inquiries about Mark's availability can be made at www.leadershipiq.com

Andrea Burgio-Murphy, Ph.D., Vice-Chairman of Leadership IQ

Andrea Burgio-Murphy, Ph.D. is the Vice-Chairman of Leadership IQ. A well-known clinical psychologist, Dr. Murphy has also served as adjunct faculty at George Washington University and on the Board of Directors of the Capitol Area Crisis Response Team in Washington, DC. She directs Consulting Services for Leadership IQ and has presented to more than a hundred groups in corporate, academic and government settings. Dr. Murphy holds a Ph.D., M.A. and B.A. from the University of Rochester.

Download free tools for managing Generation Y at:
www.generationy.net

Learn about Leadership IQ's training programs at:
www.leadershipiq.com